# BLACK HISTORY FACTS YOU DIDN'T LEARN IN SCHOOL

# Table of Contents

**Chapter One:** What You Didn't Learn about Sundown Towns ... 1

**Chapter Two:** What You Didn't Learn about the Black Communities that Prospered .......... 9

**Chapter Three:** What You Didn't Learn about Black Wall Street .......... 22

**Chapter Four:** What You Didn't Learn about Africatown .......... 25

**Chapter Five:** What You Didn't Learn about Race Riots in the United States .......... 29

**Chapter Six:** What You Didn't Learn about the Theory of Evolution .......... 37

**Chapter Seven:** What You Didn't Learn about Drapetomania ... 47

**Chapter Eight:** What You Didn't Learn about Uncle Tom ....... 52

**Chapter Nine:** What You Didn't Learn about Convict Leasing. 59

**Chapter Ten:** What You Didn't Learn about Slave Patrols ........ 64

**Chapter Eleven:** What You Didn't Learn about the State of Missouri v Celia .......... 70

**Chapter Twelve:** What You Didn't Learn about Abraham Lincoln's Colonization Plan .......... 74

**Chapter Thirteen:** What You Didn't Learn about Black History Month .......... 81

**Chapter Fourteen:** What You Didn't Learn about Lewis Howard Latimer ................................................................. 88

**Chapter Fifteen:** What You Didn't Learn about the Harriet Tubman (Mis)Quote ........................................................ 91

**Chapter Sixteen:** What You Didn't Learn about Anna Murray Douglass ........................................................................ 97

**Chapter Seventeen:** What You Didn't Learn about the Unsung Women of the Harlem Renaissance ............................. 102

**Chapter Eighteen:** What You Didn't Learn about the Chicago Black Renaissance ............................................................... 106

**Chapter Nineteen:** What You Didn't Learn about Ida B. Wells-Barnett ............................................................................. 110

**Chapter Twenty:** What You Didn't Learn about Mary Beatrice Davidson Kenner ............................................................ 114

**Chapter Twenty - One:** What You Didn't Learn about Phillip L. Downing ........................................................................ 117

**Chapter Twenty - Two:** What You Didn't Learn about the Brown Paper Bag Test ............................................................. 120

**Chapter Twenty - Three:** What You Didn't Learn about the Fultz Sisters ............................................................................. 126

**Chapter Twenty - Four:** What You Didn't Learn about Rosa Parks' Predecessors ....................................................................... 131

**Chapter Twenty - Five:** What You Didn't Learn About Dr. Martin Luther King Jr. ..................................................................... 138

**Chapter Twenty - Six:** What You Didn't Learn about A. D. King ....................................................................................... 147

**Chapter Twenty - Seven:** What You Didn't Learn about Robert Taylor ................................................................................ 151

**Chapter Twenty - Eight:** What You Didn't Learn about the Black Panther Party for Self-Defense ....................................... 157

**Chapter Twenty - Nine:** What You Didn't Learn about the Events of September 15, 1963 ................................................. 164

**Chapter Thirty:** What You Didn't Learn about Louis Till ....... 168

**Chapter Thirty - One:** What You Didn't Learn about Mostafa Hefny ............................................................................... 174

**Chapter Thirty - Two:** What You Didn't Learn about the Physical Appearance of the Ancient Israelites and Egyptians ................... 178

Afterword ................................................................................ 184

Endnotes ................................................................................. 189

# CHAPTER ONE

## What You Didn't Learn about Sundown Towns

A sundown town is an organized community that, for decades, kept African Americans from living in it[1] and was consequently all-white or mostly white (some towns allowed one or two Black families) on purpose. These communities drove out their Black residents and warned them not to return. If Blacks were to visit the town for any reason, they had to leave before the sun set or risk lynching. Many communities and suburbs today have been all-white or majority-white for decades due to this system of oppression.

"Is it true that 'Anna' stands for 'Ain't No Niggers Allowed?'" I asked at the convenience store in Anna, Illinois, where I had stopped to buy coffee.

"Yes," the clerk replied.

"That's sad. Isn't it?" she added, distancing herself from the policy. She went on to assure me that, "That all happened a long time ago."

"I understand racial exclusion is still going on?" I asked.

"Yes," she replied. "That's sad."

- James W. Loewen [2]

While sundown towns have declined over the years,[3] Anna is a good example of how these communities operated as it was common knowledge that Blacks were not allowed to live in the small Illinois town. The city was named after the daughter of its founder Anna Williard Davie but got its acronym after the 1909 lynching of William James in Cairo, Illinois.

William "Froggie" James, along with four other men, was wanted for the rape and murder of a white woman named Mary Pelley. This was not uncommon. In *100 Hundred Years of Lynchings*, Ralph Ginzburg compiled vivid newspaper accounts of racial violence committed against African Americans. Of those accounts, many of the deaths were the lynching of Black men accused of raping, speaking to, or associating in any way with white women. James's "crime" was no different, and on a cold November evening in 1909, ten thousand men, women, and children gathered to watch the death of this twenty-four-year-old Black man.[4]

Dozens of white women, not men, hung James, perhaps as a form of revenge for violating one of their own. The women pulled the rope, and under the steel arches at the intersection of Cairo's Eighth and Commercial Streets, William James dangled over the crowd.[5] Many adults carrying toddlers on their shoulders gave the impression that they were at a zoo. These children, who would one day be parents, grandparents, and great-grandparents, cheered and smiled with the approval of their parents.[6] As if hanging him before thousands of people was not enough, they lifted James high above the crowd so they could see him. The men riddled his already dead body with bullets where the city lights shone down on him. William James's body was also burned.

Following the lynching, the mob of angry white citizens drove out Anna's forty or so Black families. It was at this point that Anna, Illinois became a sundown town. According to a census report,[7] Anna was still 95.7 percent white in 2010, making it one of the whitest communities in southern Illinois.

What happened in Anna happened in many cities across the country. White people built thousands of white-only villages across the country starting around 1890 and continuing until 1968. Many municipalities put up sundown signs after driving out their Black residents.[8] Sundown towns (also called sunset towns) began after slavery and after the Civil War, when Blacks left the South and poured into every city and corner of the country. States immediately set up the system of Jim Crow. Under these laws, Blacks could not vote, drink from the same water fountain as whites, sit in the same area of the movie theater,[9] swim in the same pools and lakes, look white people in the eye when they spoke,[10] and would not be accommodated at any restaurants, parks, hotels, or schools used by whites.

While Jim Crow and segregation were notably a southern practice, these laws existed in the North too. Instead of the "Promised Land," Black migrants discovered that Jim Crow had followed them north. They could not settle in the small communities in the South. Instead, they were only permitted to settle in the oldest, most rundown areas of industrial cities. Whites fled to suburbs or urban areas with better housing.[11] Sundown towns also mainly operated in the North as the Great Migration brought floods of Blacks into northern cities. Moving into these cities caused race riots to erupt as white mobs attacked Black neighborhoods by burning them, looting, killing, and driving out the rest of their African American populations.

Cicero and Berwyn in Chicago were also sundown towns. In 1966, Dr. Martin Luther King Jr. visited Chicago due to the high poverty rate in Black neighborhoods. He stayed as part of his Poor People's Campaign[12] and rented an apartment at 1550 S. Hamlin Avenue. On that day in 1966, King and his wife, Coretta, were greeted by a broken door, dirt floors, and an "overpowering" smell of urine, according to a 2002 biography.[13] After securing the passage of the Civil Rights Act of 1964, Dr. King and his team brought their movement to "the heart of the ghetto" in Chicago, as he later wrote, to call attention to substandard housing.[14]

But that's not the only reason Dr. King and the Chicago Freedom Movement—a campaign to confront segregation and discrimination in the North—were in the city. They were also in Chicago to protest the death of Jerome Huey, a seventeen-year-old Black boy who went into Cicero for a job interview at a freight loading company when his parents' grocery store failed. Sadly, Huey never made it back. He was beaten to death by four white men with baseball bats.[15] According to Huey v. the Town of Cicero, Supreme Court of Illinois, 1968:

> The attack occurred at about 10:00 P.M. on May 25, 1966, near the intersection of 25th Place and Laramie Avenue in Cicero, Illinois, while the decedent was en route to an employment office. "That as a direct and proximate result, JEROME HUEY, was assaulted and severe injuries were inflicted * * * from which he died on May 29, 1966...the defendants, or one or more of them, were under a duty to warn, advise, or otherwise give notice to dark-skinned persons and plaintiff's intestate of the unusual and extraordinary hazards and perils to such persons as existed on May 25, 1966 in the TOWN OF CICERO." (Justia US Law, 1968)

Cicero residents were supposed to warn Black people about the dangers and risks of visiting the town. This is because many sundown towns did not explicitly state that they were sundown towns. Their status was determined by how they treated or drove out Black residents and the separatist signage they used to warn Black people to leave town.[16] These two events, housing discrimination and the death of Jerome Huey led to the march through Cicero, the all-white district on August 5, 1966. During this march, Dr. King was hit in the head with a rock by members of the angry mob. "I have never seen, even in Mississippi and Alabama, mobs as hateful as I've seen here in Chicago," Dr. King told reporters that day, stripping off his tie.[17]

However, Illinois was not the only non-southern city where sundown towns existed.

Ku Klux Klan (KKK) Grand Wizard, George Pepper and White Aryan Resistance (WAR) leader Tom Metzger claimed Fontana and the Inland Empire as their own. Additionally, Hells Angels Biker Gang originated in Fontana. Hells Angels and Nazi Low Riders (NLR) flourished in the city with no consequences from the Fontana Police Department. Many discrimination and hate crime incidents were unsolved and poorly investigated. Fontana has a long history of racism and discriminatory policies, so it is no surprise that it was also a sundown town where Blacks were not allowed south of the area. One local phrase, "Base Line is the Race Line,"[18] meant that African Americans were welcome north of Base Line Road but not to the south.

When O'Day Short, his wife, and two children moved to Fontana, California, in 1945, where the KKK had established its headquarters on land in an all-white area, neighbors threatened to leave that neighborhood. They urged the family to occupy one where the town allowed Blacks to live.

The Short family's fair skin led many to believe it was how they were able to purchase the property in the first place. The man who sold O'Day the land where they built the house did not know he was Black. Nevertheless, O'Day moved his family into the half-finished home. When people complained, O'Day received a visit from the sheriff to leave the property. The sheriff offered to repurchase the house, but O'Day refused. The sheriff then warned that the "vigilante committee" would not be pleased. They recorded the visit by the sheriff in his office in San Bernardino. According to the report, Short described the threats to the Federal Bureau of Investigation (FBI). On December 6, 1945, Short also reported the threats to the *Los Angeles Sentinel*, an African American newspaper.[19]

The Short family's house caught fire on December 16, 1945, just ten days after the reports and less than a month after they had moved in. Barry, nine, and Carol Ann, seven, were the mother's daughters; Helen Short, 35, was also killed.[20]

O'Day, who was forty years old, lived long enough to be taken to the hospital. A month later, on January 22, 1946, he also died.

An oil lamp that O'Day was lighting at the time of the tragedy has been connected to the source of the fire. However, neither in 1946 nor subsequently, when the story revived, were the reports to note that the Shorts were Black. Later, the NAACP engaged a fire investigator to check into the incident. The kerosene lamp was almost completely undamaged, according to the investigator, who concluded that someone had started the fire from the outside.[21]

## CHAPTER TWO

# What You Didn't Learn about the Black Communities that Prospered

We often hear how African Americans were sharecroppers on the farms of their previous enslavers after chattel slavery. We hear of how countless more toiled in vain to survive as strangers in a new land with no right to take part in American culture or benefit from the advantages of the American dream promised to its residents, a dream Blacks had no right to as enslaved people.

Not all Black people, nevertheless, experienced hardship following the Civil War. They didn't just accept what was given to them; many of them welcomed their newfound freedom with hope and excitement. Their aristocracy, money, or prosperity are hardly ever mentioned. This chapter delves into more detail about a few of these prosperous Black communities.

## Blackdom

Blackdom is a little-known Black community about twenty miles southwest of Roswell, New Mexico. Frank and Ella Boyer founded the town. The couple was fleeing threats from the Ku Klux Klan[1] when Blackdom, New Mexico, became the first community of African Americans in the state. Walking 2,000 miles on foot from Georgia to New Mexico, Boyer left his wife and children behind to cultivate land in the West's free territory before sending for his family three years later.

Following the Homestead Act of 1862, African Americans started to leave the South in large numbers during a movement known as "The Great Exodus," especially in Kansas. Boyer started farming after receiving a loan from the Pacific Mutual Company to drill a well. Boyer's stationery read, "Blackdom Townsite Co., Roswell, New Mexico. The only exclusive Negro settlement in New Mexico."[2]

The land was rich because of the Artesian water, which sprang in abundance and nourished it. By 1908, the town had a thriving population of 300, local businesses, and a newspaper. Boyer boasted that they had a post office, store, church, schoolhouse, pumping plant, office building, and several residents already established.[3]

Unfortunately, due to crop failures because of a drought in 1916,[4] the town's population dramatically decreased, and little remains. Although there is not much literature about the good days, the National Postal Museum acquired a small relic from the postal account book kept for Blackdom from 1912 to 1919.⁵ The money book was given to a neighboring station after the Blackdom post office closed. The book was abandoned in the back office for many years before a staffer got in touch with a postal historian, who helped the item find a new home at the Postal Museum after its previous location had been destroyed.⁶ This artifact proves this town existed and was one of many Black communities that prospered.

## Black Wall Street

There were over twenty Black communities in Oklahoma, one of its most renowned being the community of Greenwood, a neighborhood in North Tulsa, Oklahoma.

Greenwood was one of the most successful and wealthy Black communities in the United States during the early twentieth century. The town, which was dubbed "Black Wall Street" by many because of its financial success resembled that of Wall Street, also earned nicknames like "Oil Capital of the World" during the 1910s oil boom.¹ As a result, the area of northeast Oklahoma around Tulsa flourished, including the Greenwood neighborhood. Home to several prominent Black businesspeople, the community held many multimillionaires. Viola Fletcher, then 107 years old, spoke on her family's experience of that day one hundred years after the slaughter. She said, "I went to bed at my family's house in Greenwood. The neighborhood I slept in that night was wealthy, not only financially, but also culturally and historically. I was secure. I had all the necessities for a child. I saw a promising future."²

Before its destruction, Black Wall Street was the promised land for Black Americans who had fled the captivity of the Pharaohs of the South. Due to the segregation laws that kept Black people from networking with white businessmen and women, the residents of Greenwood pooled their resources to establish Black businesses. As a result, the community became a robust and self-sustaining hub of barbershops, clothing stores, restaurants, movie theaters, jewelers, taverns, pool houses, grocery stores, newspapers, doctors' offices, schools, mansion homes, and much more. The Greenwood community did so well that the dollar circulated thirty-six to one-hundred times.[3] This means it took up to a full year before the dollar left the community.

While we cannot substantiate the claim from the NAACP and other organizations that the dollar in the Black community leaves the neighborhood in six hours,[4] the Black dollar is extremely limited today compared to 100 years ago.

The Greenwood community of North Tulsa was significant not only in its prosperity, but also in its founding. For this, we give it its own chapter in that we may dig deeper into its origin, its thriving, and its downfall.

## Boley

In Oklahoma, after the Civil War, it was common for former slaves of Native Americans to settle together following the Trail of Tears.[1] Likewise, freed slaves learned about land opportunities through local newspapers.[2] In mass, African Americans established communities in Oklahoma advertised in all-Black newspapers as "a wonderful place with rich soil, great land, and great opportunities."[3] Between 1856 and 1920, many all-Black towns were established, positioning the city as a place of opportunity for Black Americans.[4]

A day before Oklahoma became a state, *The Muskogee Cimeter*, a Black-owned newspaper, ran an article notifying Blacks that Oklahoma and the Indian Territory were now states and that thousands of acres of land were available for lease and rent. Because of ads like this, the all-Black community of Boley, Oklahoma, was founded in 1904. According to the Oklahoma Historical Society, Boley flourished after Lake Moore, vice president of the railroad, wanted to establish a depot there because he believed residents could govern themselves.[5] It established itself as a self-governing town — by Blacks, for Blacks — and boasted over 5,000 citizens at one point.[6] Head said of Boley. "They had everything that Chicago or any other burgeoning town had."[7] With railroad access and land, Boley became one of at least twenty Black towns in Oklahoma to thrive. By 1907, it had at least 1,000 residents and twice that many farmers settled outside of town. There were several businesses and an industrial school.

Not that operating on the same level as white banks gave it credibility, but by owning and operating the first Black-owned bank to receive a national charter, Boley's residents accomplished something that America could not ignore. Boley even attracted the attention of Booker T. Washington, who visited on occasion, calling it "the most enterprising and in many ways the most interesting Negro town in the United States."⁸

## Eatonville

Eatonville is the hometown of renowned author, folklorist, anthropologist, and filmmaker Zora Neale Hurston. Zora Hurston, who was three when her family moved to the town in 1894, always thought of it as her birthplace.

Located six miles north of Orlando in Orange County, Florida, Eatonville is one of the oldest Black-incorporated municipalities in the United States. The Emancipation of 1863 was followed by ratifying the 13th, 14th, and 15th amendments, which inspired newly freed Blacks to create their own municipal corporations. (It would take an entire book to cover all the towns freed Black people built.) Between 1864 and 1900, there were more than 400 Black towns, settlements, and enclaves. According to the president of the Association to Preserve the Eatonville Community, "The town was founded as a black haven."."¹

In the 1888 *Eatonville Speaker* newspaper, the town promoted the community to recruit Black people into moving to the area with this ad: "Colored people of the United States! Solve the great race problem by securing a home in Eatonville, Florida, a negro city governed by negroes."² Blacks flocked to Eatonville. The town also became famous due to Zora Neale Hurston, who talked about the community in her work, namely, *Their Eyes Were Watching God.*

The people built one-story wood-frame houses and set aside land for clubhouses, cemeteries, and municipal buildings. There were nearby lakes to cook, bathe, and irrigate crops. Some men found work building new railroads, and others started their own businesses. Women found work as cooks, started vegetable gardens, or worked as maids of nearby towns. There were storeowners and builders. Eatonville also became home to the area's best school for Black children, the Robert Hungerford Industrial School.[3]

If that were not enough, perhaps Eatonville's greatest legacy is that, unlike the other communities that were destroyed, Eatonville still exists today.

## Fort Mose

Fort Mose was the first free Black community in what is now the Unites States, and it was situated north of St. Augustine, Florida. In what would become one of the first Emancipation Proclamations, King Charles II ordered that any enslaved man who escaped from an English plantation to Florida would be freed if he joined the militia and converted to Catholicism.[1] This was done to undermine British colonization. Due to its proximity to the English colony of South Carolina, Spanish Florida served as a haven for escaped slaves.[2]

By 1738, there were hundreds of Blacks, mostly runaways from the Carolinas, living in what became Fort Mose. These runaways were skilled workers, blacksmiths, carpenters, cattlemen, boatmen, and farmers. Black settlers created a colony of freed people with accompanying women and children that ultimately attracted other fugitive slaves.

## Israel Hill

Settled in Prince Edward County, Virginia, this community was established in 1810-1811 by ninety formerly enslaved men and women. These freedmen gained their freedom and 350 acres from Judith Randolph under her husband, Richard Randolph, who left her the land in his will. Richard was also the young cousin of Thomas Jefferson.[1] These free Blacks, who referred to themselves as Israelites,[2] worked as farmers, craftspeople, and Appomattox River boatmen. Some labored alongside whites for equal wages, and the family of early settler Hercules White bought and sold real estate in Farmville. Israel Hill remained a vibrant Black community into the twentieth century. As with many Black communities that prospered, Israel Hill was not without existing discrimination. Its occupants were disparaged by pro-slavery activists both locally and internationally, even though it appeared that interactions between free Blacks and whites in the region were peaceful.[3] Things were not perfect, but this does not take away from what these freedmen built.

## Mound Bayou

The first all-Black town in Mississippi, Mound Bayou, was founded by two formerly enslaved men, Isaiah Montgomery and his cousin, Benjamin Green. According to a July 1887, Cleveland, Mississippi article, in December of 1886, Montgomery and Green bought 840 acres of land from the Louisville-New Orleans & Texas Railroad for seven dollars an acre.[1] That acreage would serve as the site of Mound Bayou, but it wouldn't be easy. The terrain was said to be covered in a thick layer of trees and bushes, and the only way to travel through it was with a hatchet or machete. Wild animals abounded in the woodlands, and swamp fever—to which some settlers fell victim—was a constant source of worry. But, the guys did manage to locate some settlers, and they erected a shop for supplies, a sawmill, and a post office; they acquired a cotton gin, and even started a school.[2]

Mound Bayou reached a population of 4,000 people (99.6 percent Black) by 1907.[3] The community also had a train depot, a bank, numerous thriving industries, various stores and eateries, a newspaper, a telephone exchange, and eventually, a hospital. "It was an effort made to find you a place where you could govern yourselves and work for yourself versus working for the master or working for someone else. That was attractive to people, especially to those that had experienced slavery," said Eulah Peterson, Mayor of Mound Bayou. Peterson's grandfather, a former slave, moved to Mound Bayou in 1903.[4]

The Great Depression of the 1930s devastated the town,[5] but Mound Bayou was a flourishing Black community before that.

## Nicodemus Township

The United States bought the land of the territory that would become the state of Kansas as part of the Louisiana Purchase of 1803. The Missouri Compromise intended for Kansas to be a state where Black people would be free. In 1861, Kansas adopted an anti-slavery constitution that many settlers saw as a land of opportunity after the Civil War. During this "Colored Exodus," thousands of African Americans left the South looking for new lands, and many of them headed for Kansas.

Nicodemus was founded in 1877 by seven members, six of whom were Black along the south fork of the Solomon River. Benjamin "Pap" Singleton, a former enslaved man and Underground Railroad conductor, helped produce the "Kansas Fever" of the late 1870s. Tens of thousands of African Americans left their homes headed for Singleton's Cherokee County colony or Nicodemus in Graham County, Kansas. In April 1877, before officially registering the town, the Nicodemus Town Company began advertising the community in Lexington and Georgetown, Kentucky, extolling Nicodemus as "The Largest Colored Colony in America."[1]

According to the Nicodemus National Historical Society, Nicodemus was the first Black community west of the Mississippi River and is the only predominantly Black community west of the Mississippi that remains a living community today.[2] The first wave of settlers, 350 people strong, arrived on September 17, 1877. Promoted as the "Promised Land" throughout the South, founders hosted visits by potential settlers.[2] The town's success, like many communities, was due to the agricultural economy, which yielded decent profits for farmers.

By 1910, 600 residents lived there. Although the town was a mixture of white and Black, most residents were Black, and the town of Nicodemus became the center of Black culture. The Great Depression, coupled with the community's reliance on railroads, dealt a blow to the town, but Nicodemus remained a thriving African American community through World War I.

## Rosewood

When the late John Singleton made a movie starring Ving Rhames about an all-black community in 1997, the forgotten legacy of Rosewood was remembered.

Settled by Blacks and whites in 1845, Jim Crow and Black codes forced a separation of the races in the years after the Civil War. By the 1920s, Rosewood's population was predominantly African American except for one white family who ran a general store.[1] The quiet town prospered in 1870 when they set up a railway depot to transport the abundant red cedar, from which the city got its name, from Rosewood to a pencil factory in Cedar Key. By 1900, the community was predominantly Black with a school, turpentine mill, baseball team, general store, and sugarcane mill. The neighborhood had two dozen plank-story homes, some other small houses, and several small unoccupied plank structures.

Fannie Taylor, a white woman, had been assaulted. Consequently, she escalated the situation by claiming a Black man raped her. As a result, in January of 1923, white mobs burned the town down.

However, before the massacre, the city of Rosewood was a thriving Black community.

## Seneca Village

Seneca Village was settled in the 1820s on the eve of Emancipation in New York. The only community of Black property in the city at the time, it was located between 82nd and 87th Street east of what is now Central Park. The Village had its own school and a population of over 250 people. Citizens built houses on the land, some of them elaborate two-story homes with barns.

We were not taught in school that Black people were not only held as slaves in the South. More than 42 percent of New York City households had slaves in 1703, and slavery played a significant role in the growth of the city. Up to 20 percent of New Yorkers were Blacks who were held as slaves.[1] Nearly every businessman in 18th-century New York had a role in the trafficking of human beings at some point. Only Charleston, South Carolina could compete with New York in terms of how deeply slavery permeated society.[2] Differences in the life of enslaved persons in the North might mean that instead of plantations, the enslaved slept in cellars and attics or above farmhouse kitchens in the country. New York City's enslaved population was emancipated in 1827, and many of these freedmen comprised the residents of Seneca Village.

A twenty-five-year-old Black shoe shiner, Andrew Williams, bought the first three lots of land from John and Elizabeth Whitehead for $125. Epiphany Davis, a store clerk, bought twelve lots for $578, and the AME Zion Church purchased another six lots. From there, a community was born.[3] Despite New York State's abolition of slavery in 1827, discrimination against African Americans was still prevalent, and opportunities for Blacks were severely limited. Seneca Village provided a refuge from that world. Residents of Seneca Village also thrived and lived more stable lives compared to other Blacks in the city. For African American men to be eligible to vote in New York State in 1821, they had to own at least $250 worth of property and have lived there for at least three years. Ten of the one-hundred Black New Yorkers who were eligible to vote did so in Seneca Village in 1845.[4] By 1855, half of Seneca Village residents owned their homes. With homeownership came the right to vote.

The Village's demise came with the building of what is now Central Park. The government claimed the land under the right of eminent domain and evicted the residents; consequently, Seneca Village faded into the background.

# CHAPTER THREE

## What You Didn't Learn about Black Wall Street

On June 1, 1921, North Tulsa, Oklahoma, also known as "Little Africa," was the victim of systematic destruction. Although it was a model community that took years to build, it lay fuming—the city was destroyed, and mansions were melted down to the ground. The residents' hope stretched their mournful arms forward in a desperate attempt to hold on to its dear Greenwood.

The story began the same way most racist tragedies do—with a Black man accused of accosting a white woman. *The Tulsa Tribune* reported on May 31, 1921, that Dick Rowland, a Black man, tried to rape Sarah Page, a white woman. Unprecedented racial violence broke out over the course of two days as a result of local whites' refusal to wait for the investigation to progress. Thirty-five city blocks caught fire, resulting in 300 fatalities and 800 injuries.[1]

This was the beginning of what culminated in the destruction of Black Wall Street.

Greenwood was a neighborhood in Tulsa, Oklahoma, and one of the most successful and wealthy Black communities in the United States during the early twentieth century. It was popularly known as America's "Black Wall Street" because its financial success mirrored the Wall Street of Lower Manhattan. Home to several prominent Black businesspeople, the community held many multimillionaires.

The community boasted a variety of thriving businesses that were very successful up until the Tulsa Race Massacre. Not only did Blacks want to contribute to the success of their own shops, but also the racial segregation laws prevented them from shopping anywhere other than Greenwood, a mecca of opportunity to build up what Black people had been denied access to. Instead of complaining about how they were not included in the all-white newspaper, they created two of their own. Blacks were discouraged from using the new Carnegie Library downtown for whites, so they built their own smaller all-Black branch library. Not stressing over being left out of restaurants, grocery stores, and public schools, they made their own on the backs of a drive toward honest entrepreneurship.[2] Clothes bought at Elliot & Hooker's clothing at 124 N. Greenwood could be fitted across the street at H. L. Byars' tailor shop at 105 N.

Greenwood, and then cleaned around the corner at Hope Watson's cleaners at 322 E. Archer. The dollar in this community rotated thirty-six to 100 times. This meant it took up to 100 rotations before the dollar left this community.

Following the massacre, the area was rebuilt, but it was not the same.³ The community did well until the 1960s, when integration permitted Blacks to shop in once restricted areas.

# CHAPTER FOUR

## What You Didn't Learn about Africatown

On March 2, 1807, the United States Congress approved an act prohibiting importing slaves from any foreign kingdom, place, or country into any port or site within the jurisdiction of the United States, banning the Slave Trade.[1] A group of slaveholders then made a bet that they could still import slaves without being caught. Steamboat captain Timothy Meaher then smuggled 110 people from Dahomey (now Benin).[2]

The African tribes were at war, and the conquering tribes sold the members of the conquered tribes into slavery. Dahomey warriors raided the Tarkbar tribe's settlement near the city of Tamale, and the survivors were brought to Whydah, now the People's Republic of Benin, and sold. At Whydah, the captured tribesmen were sold for $100 each.³ They were taken and held captive aboard the Clotilde, commonly known as the Clotilda, the last known slave ship to bring captives from Africa to America. The Clotilda was a two-masted wooden ship built and owned by the wealthy mobile shipper and shipyard owner Meaher and docked in Mobile, Alabama, in July of 1860.⁴ The enslaved were removed from the ship and put on a steam riverboat, and the Clotilda was burned in the Mobile Bay to hide the evidence. It was lost to history in the muddy waters of the bay until May 22, 2019, when the Alabama Historical Commission and partners announced that the wreck had been located.⁵

Since the shipwreck was discovered four years ago, there has been renewed interest in the Clotilda survivors and the community they established after their liberation.

The enslaved were divided between the men who made the bet, but they eventually got caught. Federal authorities prosecuted the men, but the 1861 federal court case of US v. Byrnes Meaher, Timothy Meaher, and John Dabey was thrown out because of lack of evidence.⁶ After the Civil War, Meaher freed his slaves and allowed them to work his property. This was the beginning of the community of Africatown.⁷

Through the Slave Wrecks Project, the National Museum of African American History and Culture joined the endeavor to find the Clotilda in 2018. The museum, and SWP assisted the Alabama Historical Commission in archaeological work and in developing a method to include the Africatown community in the process of preserving the memory of the Clotilda and the past of slavery and freedom in Alabama.[8] Additionally, the Diving with a Purpose (DWP) organization, a group that trains divers to find and conserve historical and cultural artifacts buried deep in the waters, are responsible for training some of the divers' part of the mission to discover the Clotilda.[9]

Many of Africatown's citizens are descendants of the Africans who were brought to Alabama on the Clotilda and have preserved the town's history.

In April, 2023, we had the privilege of visiting the Africatown community. Near the AfricaTown bridge sits a fifteen-foot highway wall with a mural of the Clotilda. It was painted by Mr. Labbaron Lewis, a kind man who does not shy away from pictures. "I'm not a tyrant," he says, laughing when asked if we could film.[10] He wears black jeans and a white t-shirt, both splattered with paint. His straw hat covers his head as beads of sweat trickle down his face. He is hard at work painting when we arrive, and his glasses protect his eyes from the sun. He says it took him seven years to paint the wall, and he is repainting it.

Now bound by railroad tracks on one side and water on the other, there is hardly any business in Africatown, only abandoned buildings, heavy industry, and a busy highway that runs through the heart of the area. A cemetery sits on a hill along the roadway, with gravestones pointing east toward Africa. It is the resting place of the Clotilda's descendants and their descendants.

The National Museum of African American History and Culture continues to work directly with the descendant community in Africatown to develop educational, preservation, and outreach opportunities with the community. The Africatown Heritage House was scheduled to open on on July 8, 2023, the 163rd anniversary of the community's founders arriving in the United States in shackles.

A community building will house "Clotilda: The Exhibition," to share this long-untold story. The Mobile County Commission created the facility. However, a collaborative initiative with numerous entities working in collaboration with the community has brought this museum to life. This includes the Alabama Historical Commission, which is leading the scientific efforts surrounding the search for, authentication and protection of the ship Clotilda and related artifacts, and the History Museum of Mobile, which curated, constructed, and funded "Clotilda: The Exhibition" with generous support from other local organizations.[11]

# CHAPTER FIVE

## What You Didn't Learn about Race Riots in the United States

Racial violence in the form of riots and massacres that drove Black residents out of their neighborhoods, leaving these towns mostly all-white, was one of the factors contributing to the growth of the sundown towns discussed in chapter one. Several of these riots are discussed in this chapter.

### New Orleans Riot, 1886

On July 30, 1886, white men attacked Blacks parading outside the Mechanics Institute in New Orleans, where a reconvened Louisiana Constitutional Convention was held. Republicans in Louisiana had called for the convention due to the legislature's enactment of the Black Codes.[1]

## Wilmington North Carolina, 1898

When D. W. Griffith's 1915 film *Birth of a Nation* portrayed Black men as savages seeking to rape white women, contrasted against the positive portrayal of the KKK, it produced a second wave of the organization that began in Atlanta, Georgia.[2] It quickly spread to a peak membership of millions by the 1920s. Thus, when a prominent Black newspaper editor named Alex Manly wrote an editorial suggesting that relations between white women and Black men were consensual, 500 white men burned Manly's office, and fourteen African Americans were killed in the riot which has also been called a massacre, rebellion, revolt, race war, and coup d'etat.[3]

## East St. Louis, 1917

On July 1, 1917, a Black man was rumored to have killed a white man. A riot followed with whites shooting, beating, and lynching African Americans. The violence continued for a week, and the deaths ranged from forty to 200. As a result, some 6,000 Blacks fled St. Louis.[4]

## Red Summer, 1919

1919 was referred to as *Red Summer* because of the mass blood spill of race riots that year. Twenty-six cities experienced riots, including, but not limited to: Longview, TX; Washington, D. C.; Knoxville, TN; Omaha, NE, and Chicago, IL.[5] In 1919, racial tensions were exceptionally high in the North. Chicago experienced the most violence when on July 27, 1919, seventeen-year-old Eugene Williams was swimming with his friends in Lake Michigan and entered a "whites only" area. White men threw rocks at Williams, who drowned from blows to the head. After police refused to arrest the murderer, fights between white and Black gangs became the spark that started a race riot that lasted through August 3rd. It escalated so that Illinois had to call in the state militia.[6]

## Harlem Race Riot, 1943

From August 1st through 2nd, 1943, a race riot broke out in Harlem, New York, when officer James Collins shot and wounded Robert Bandy, a Black soldier. This was one of six riots that year related to Black and white tensions during World War II.[7]

## Michigan, 1943

Considered one of the worst race riots of WWII, The Detroit Riot of 1943 started with a fist fight. Racial tensions were already high due to confrontations between white and Blacks when the Sojourner Truth Housing Projects opened (1942) in a white neighborhood, and whites tried to stop Blacks from moving in.[8]

A fight broke out at the Belle Isle Amusement Park in the Detroit River and turned into a fight between whites and Blacks and spilled over into the streets. The violence ended when 6,000 federal troops were ordered into the city. Twenty-five Blacks and nine whites were reportedly killed, with seventeen Blacks killed by the police.[9]

## The Groveland Four, 1949

On July 16, 1949, a white couple's car stopped on a rural road in Groveland, Florida. The next day, seventeen-year-old Norma

Padgett accused four Black men of raping her.[10] Sheriffs arrested Charles Greenlee, Sam Shepherd, and Walter Irvin. The fourth man, Ernest Thomas, fled the county and was hunted down and killed by a mob of over 1,000 armed sheriffs.[11] When word spread about the arrest of "The Groveland Four," an angry crowd of white Klansmen surrounded the jail, and the men were hidden and transported to Raiford State Prison. The mob was not pleased. They went on to attack the Black section of Groveland, a small town in South Lake County where two of the accused men's families lived. Black residents were urged to leave town, and the National Guard was called in. Meanwhile, they severely beat the accused men; Shepherd and Irvin were sentenced to death; and Greenlee was given life in prison because of his age. Sheriff Willis McCall of Lake County shot Shepherd and Irvin while they were being transported to a pretrial hearing in 1951 when they retried the case. He claimed that the men in handcuffs were attempting to run.[12]

Seventy-two years later, in November of 2021, Florida officials dismissed the rape charge in their case.[13]

## Los Angeles, 1965

The Watts Riots occurred between August 11th-17th after a white patrolman arrested twenty-one-year-old Marquette Frye, a Black motorist. A fight involving Frye, his brother, his mother, and the police broke out. Police arrested his mother and brother, and the number of people gathered increased. Almost 4,000 National Guardsmen were deployed, in addition to approximately 1,600 police officers.[14] Martial law was declared, and the city issued a curfew. More than 30,000 people participated in the riots, fighting with police, looting white-owned homes and businesses, and attacking white residents. The riots left thirty-four dead, more than 1,000 injured, and approximately 4,000 arrested.[15]

## New Jersey, 1967

On July 12, 1967, a Black cab driver, John Smith, was arrested for illegally passing a police car. He was taken to a police station across the street from the projects. These residents reported that the police beat this man and dragged him from the cab into the station. Word got to civil rights leaders who organized a protest, but the protest turned violent. Rioting followed for several nights, and the National Guard was deployed. Even with the National Guard present, rioting continued.[16]

## MLK Riots, 1968

After losing leaders like Malcolm X and Medgar Evers, the outcry in the Black community over the assassination of Dr. Martin Luther King Jr., was monumental. Riots broke out in 125 cities following the April 4, 1968 assassination.[17] The worst occurred in Baltimore, Washington D. C., and Chicago. On April 5, looting, arson, and attacks on police increased, and as many as 20,000 people participated in the riots. The National Guard and Marines were dispatched. The riots reached within two blocks of the White House; twelve people were killed, and more than 1,200 buildings were destroyed.[18]

## Crown Heights Race Riots, 1991

On August 21, 1991, in the Crown Heights neighborhood of Brooklyn, New York, a car driven by Yosef Lifsh hit another vehicle and then crashed into two seven-year-old Black children. Residents of Crown Heights gathered and began attacking Lifsh and other Hasidic Jews. A city ambulance crew and the Hasidic-run Hatzolah ambulance service arrived. The Hatzolah service brought injured Jews to the hospital, and the city crew transported the Black children. Gavin Cato, one of the Black children, died. African American residents felt the Jews were given preferential medical treatment and began throwing rocks and bottles at police and the homes and businesses of Hasidic Jews. The riots raged for three days. More than 150 officers and approximately forty civilians were injured in the rioting.[19]

## Rodney King Riots, 1992

On March 3, 1991, Rodney King was pulled over for driving recklessly, and someone videotaped the encounter with the police from his apartment balcony. The video showed the officers severely beating Rodney. On April 29, 1992, a jury acquitted three officers, and predominantly Black areas of Los Angeles erupted in violence. Six days of riots led to fifty deaths, thousands of arrests, and an estimated one billion dollars in property damage.[20]

## Ferguson, Missouri, 2014

On August 9, 2014, officer Darren Wilson shot and killed Michael Brown, an unarmed eighteen-year-old teenager in Ferguson,

Missouri. Details of the shooting have been under dispute since the incident. Police said that Brown was shot during an altercation with Wilson. However, a friend of Brown said that Wilson shot Brown when he refused to move from the middle of the street and that Brown's hands were over his head at the moment of the shooting. The following night, protesters filled the streets near the shooting. Police officers arrived on the scene with riot gear, including rifles and shields. The protest turned violent, and images from cell phones went viral on social media, including several accounts of looting.[21]

## Maryland, 2015

Freddie Gray, a twenty-five-year-old Black man, died of a severe spinal cord injury, while in police custody.[22] After his funeral, angry residents took to the streets of Northwest Baltimore to protest. Governor Larry Hogan declared a state of emergency, called in the National Guard, and set a curfew as rocks were thrown and cinder blocks, buildings, and cars were set on fire.[23]

## Minneapolis and Cities Globally, 2020

On May 25, 2020, George Floyd, a forty-six-year-old Black man, was arrested and subsequently killed in Minneapolis, Minnesota after being handcuffed and pinned to the ground by Derek Chauvin, a white police officer. Bystanders captured video of the officer behind a police car using his knee to pin Floyd by his neck, leaning on him for nine minutes and twenty-nine seconds despite his cries of the inability to breathe.[24] This death led to a global outcry over police brutality against Black men. While these were more protests rather than riots, the extent of the demonstrations was historical, with protests erupting in at least 140 cities across the United States, activating the National Guard in at least twenty-one states, and protests in several other countries.[25]

# CHAPTER SIX

## What You Didn't Learn about the Theory of Evolution

The original title for Charles Darwin's *Origins of Species*, published on November 24, 1859, (selling out on the first day), was *On the Origins of Species by Means of Natural Selection, or The Preservation of Favoured Races in the Struggle for Life.*[1]

Also referred to as "survival of the fittest," with the theory of evolution, Darwin suggested that organisms adapt to their environments to help better them to survive and reproduce. The cousin of Charles Darwin, Francis Galton, took Darwin's philosophies and ideas on evolution and put them into practice in what became known as eugenics, from the Greek word *eugenes*, meaning "well-born."[2] The phrase "well-born" has two connotations: born healthy and born wealthy. The impoverished, the illiterate, criminals, recent immigrants, Blacks, and the feebleminded were viewed as eugenic misfits; white, well-educated people of excellent social class were deemed eugenically superior.[3]

Eugenics is a racist scientific process that set out to prove the inferiority of Blacks through alleged psychological and medical evidence. Galton proposed that the poor, the sick, the weak, and the "untalented" should be prevented from multiplying.[4] He maintained that the principle of the "survival of the fittest" had to be complied with and that only the strongest should be allowed to participate in the world.[5] Galton said that the average Black person lacked the intelligence, independence, and self-control necessary to carry the weight of any decent type of civilization without a significant amount of outside direction and assistance.[6]

Eugenics and evolution are related in that they drew a correlation between the highest animal in the primate world—the gorilla, and what was seen as the lowest mammal in the human world—the African.[7] Galton's racists ideas derived from his visits to areas of southwest Africa in the early 1850s. He remarked several times on the effect this had on his work. Addressing the Royal Society in 1886, on being awarded their medal, Galton gave a typical vivid summary: "I saw enough of savage races to give me material to think about all the rest of my life."[8]

In the early 1900s, a businessman in slave trading named Samuel Verner, tasked with acquiring pygmies for a cultural evolution display at the Louisiana Purchase Exposition in St. Louis, Missouri, encountered a man named Ota Benga, a Congolese Mbuti or Bambuti, one of several indigenous pygmy groups in the Congo region of Africa.[9] Paid by the St. Louis Exposition Company a year earlier to hunt men instead of monkeys, he was to bring African pygmies to America for the St. Louis World Fair. A Belgium militia group who set out to control the natives of that land for the ample supply of rubber in the Congo killed Benga's family. Benga survived because he was on a hunting mission, until he was kidnapped and taken to the United States by Samuel.[10]

Benga's physical appearance, as most Mbuti, astonished onlookers who immediately compared him to an animal, specifically for his short stature and razor-sharp teeth. Displays of humans were widespread in the early twentieth century to prove the theory of the evolution of man. Black men and women from the eastern part of the world were used as examples of the lower class of humans and often displayed. They were usually men and women with abnormal features. With Benga's appearance, he and his fellow men became an instant attraction, and the men attracted spectators wherever they went until he was eventually caged at a Bronx Zoo in 1906.[11]

On May 20, 1916, Ota Benga put a gun to his heart and pulled the trigger.

Nineteenth-century scientists were convinced that the white race was superior to other races and that they could find this superiority in Darwinian theory. One key person in perpetuating this was Thomas Huxley, an English biologist, and anthropologist specializing in comparative anatomy and known as "Darwin's Bulldog" for his advocacy of Darwin's theory of evolution.[12] Huxley contends that no sane person who is aware of the facts thinks the average Black person is better than the typical white person, let alone equal to him.[13] For eugenicists, the white race had moved up the evolutionary ladder and was destined to eliminate other races in the struggle to survive.

When twenty-year-old Sara Saartjie Baartman, also known by the stage name "Hottentot Venus," embarked on a boat from Cape Town to London in 1810, she could not have known that she would never see South Africa again. Nor, as she stood on the deck and saw what had become her home disappear behind her, could she have known that she would become the icon of racial inferiority and Black female sexuality for the next one hundred years.

A Khoisan woman from South Africa, Baartman's large buttocks astonished Europeans, and she was forced to sing and dance before crowds and onlookers. Londoners stared at Venus's large bottom as she turned around on stage and they pondered the size of other parts that were concealed from view.[14] Baartman was made to perform a naked dance, and for an additional fee, you could poke her with a stick or your fingers.[15] They also put this young woman in a cage (as they did Benga), poking, prodding, and groping her. Her protruding buttocks were regarded as disgusting, indecent, and obscene. She had steatopygia, a disorder that typically affects people in desert areas of southern Africa.[16] She also had elongated labia; a physical feature derogatorily referred to as a "Hottentot apron."[17]

Baartman is another example of racist and pseudo-scientific theories regarding Black inferiority and the hyper sexualization of the Black woman. Baartman's features were exoticized as a result of how significantly they deviated from prevalent notions of white feminine beauty.[18] White men made Black women seem inferior because of their shapes. Ironically, white women historically wore quilted petticoats, farthingales, and bum rolls that were specifically designed to make their butts look bigger.[19] Baartman's voluptuous and curvaceous body—mocked and shamed in the West—was also described in advertisements as the "most correct and perfect specimen of her race."[20]

Baartman's predicament drew the attention of Robert Wedderburn, a young Jamaican who was fed up with slavery and racism. Subsequently, his group pressured the attorney general to stop the humiliation of Baartman. Losing the case on a technicality, Baartman spent four years in London and then went to Paris where she was exhibited in a traveling circus and seen frequently controlled by an animal trainer in the show. Here, she crossed paths with George Cuvier, Napoleon's surgeon general, who became the Dean of Comparative Anatomy. In his capacity as a social anthropologist, he concluded that Baartman was the missing link. He also made a plaster cast of her body when she died prior to dissecting it. Cuvier removed her skeleton and cut out her brain and her genitals, which he put on display.[21]

Sarah Baartman died poor in 1816, and her organs, including her genitals and brains, were preserved in bottles of formaldehyde. Her remains were displayed at the Musée de L'Homme in Paris until as late as 1974.[22]

Shocking as this is, these practices of exploitation of the Black body were nothing new.

Joice Heth was an enslaved Black woman who P.T. Barnum, a famous showman and museum owner, purchased in 1835 and claimed she was the 161-year-old "Mammy" of George Washington.[23] Heth had gone through a few hands. Barnum bought her from R. W. Lindsay of Kentucky who had purchased her earlier that year from John S. Bowling. Bowling was the first to market Heth as an elderly woman with an alleged connection to Washington. Like Benga and Baartman, Heth's physical appearance helped make Barnum's deceptions about her extreme old age seem more plausible to his racist audiences.

Barnum paraded the blind and nearly paralyzed Joice Heth across New England from August 1835 to February 1836 advertising her as "the Greatest Natural and National Curiosity in the World."[24] The public described her as "weighing forty-six pounds," and noted that she "was also blind and had no teeth."[25] One observer wrote that "[Heth] is a mere skeleton covered with skin, and her whole appearance very much resembles a mummy of the days of the Pharaohs, taken entire from the catacombs of Egypt."[26]

Barnum advertised Heth as one would a circus animal in newspapers to announce their shows. One broadside promoting Barnum's 1835 show described Heth, his new attraction, as "unquestionably the most astonishing and interesting curiosity in the world...and...the first person who put cloths [*sic*] on the unconscious infant who was destined to lead our heroic fathers on to glory, to victory, and to freedom."[27] New York City newspapers carried the following obituary on February 24, 1836:

"Yesterday departed this life, at the great age of One Hundred and Sixty-Two Years, JOICE HETH, stated to have been the Nurse of George Washington."[28]

As a result, Benga, Baartman, and Heth were not considered human beings. Instead, they were treated as if they were gorillas and were shown to be inferior to white people.

Elite African Americans are not to be excluded from this conversation. Many prominent Blacks also supported eugenics. Fisk University's first Black president and critical contributor to the Harlem Renaissance, Charles S. Johnson, said that "eugenic discrimination was necessary for blacks,"[29] and that "the high maternal and infant mortality rates, along with diseases like tuberculosis, typhoid, malaria, and venereal infection, made it difficult for large families to adequately sustain themselves."[30]

Johnson later became an integral part of Margaret Sanger's Negro Project, which was an implicit drive to "exterminate the Negro population" through religion.[31]

In a letter, Sanger outlined her plan to reach out to Black leaders—specifically ministers—to help dispel community suspicions about the family planning clinics she was opening in the South.[32] "The mass of ignorant Negros still breed carelessly and disastrously," said NAACP founder W.E.B. Dubois in the *Birth Control Review*, "so that the increase among Negroes," he went on, "even more than the increase among whites, is from that portion of the population least intelligent and fit, and least able to rear their children properly."[33]

Dr. Dubois asserted that the Black community was open to "intelligent propaganda of any sort," and "the American Birth Control League and other agencies ought to get their speakers before church congregations and their arguments in the Negro newspapers."[34]

The campaign worked. Black pastors invited Sanger to speak to their congregations, and Black publications like the *Afro-American* and *The Chicago Defender* featured her writings. Even Dr. King was awarded The Margaret Sanger Award in 1966.[35]

The Margaret Sanger Research Bureau (MSRB) operated under several names and parent organizations between 1923 and 1974. Sanger merged the Southern Clinics, the Clinical Research Bureau, and the American Birth Control League to form the Birth Control Federation of America (BCFA) and recruited Black leadership like Dubois. Soon, BCFA clinics started popping up in poor Black neighborhoods. Subsequently, the birth control industry was substituted with planned parenthood in the bylaws of the BCFA, which was renamed the Planned Parenthood Federation of America.[36]

The first Planned Parenthood clinic was the Bethlehem Centers in urban Nashville, Tennessee, where Blacks constituted only 25 percent of the population, and no one made more than fifteen dollars a week. The center opened on February 13, 1940, and the second opened in rural Berkeley County, South Carolina. The organization chose the site because South Carolina had been the second state to limit the number of children in its state public health program after a survey revealed that 25 percent of infant deaths occurred in mothers deemed unfit for pregnancy.[37]

Eugenics also included forced sterilization.

In 1907, Indiana passed the world's first eugenics-based mandatory sterilization law.[38] They targeted the poor, the mentally disabled, and Black people, and used words like "poverty-stricken," "imbecile," and "urban welfare." These groupings represented individuals who were not the highly educated members of the social elite that eugenicists regarded as being among the well-born, wealthy, and in good health. They were eugenic misfits, and by the turn of the century, eugenicists claimed that by preventing these groups from reproducing, the inherited condition of "feeblemindedness" could be eradicated.[39] While poor whites were also considered mentally unfit (many of them sent to asylums sometimes called "idiot schools"),[40] the term disproportionately affected the African American community, until eventually, *feebleminded* and *poverty-*

*stricken* were code words for Black people. After the controversial Buck v. Bell case legalized forced sterilization, twenty-seven states had passed similar legislation for the mentally impaired, welfare recipients, and people with genetic deformities by 1935.[41]

Physicians and scientists were dependent on slavery not only for economic reasons but also for clinical material. Even after chattel slavery had ended, racist scientists put people like Ota Benga, Saartjie Baartman, Joice Heth, and many others on display to argue the inferiority of Black people. To support these claims was the pseudo-science of eugenics, rooted in Charles Darwin's theory of evolution.

# CHAPTER SEVEN

## What You Didn't Learn about Drapetomania

Dr. Samuel A. Cartwright was a prominent physician and medical writer in New Orleans who specialized in "mental alienation," an expression that meant a break with reality or a schism in mind. Also known as "Free Negro Insanity," Cartwright defined "drapetomania" as the madness of enslaved Blacks running away from their white captors. He derived this term from the Greek words *drapeto*, meaning "runaway slave," and mania, meaning "mad" or "crazy."[1]

Cartwright believed that Blacks who rebelled did so because of mental instability. He thought that with the proper medical advice and treatment, they could prevent the practice of the enslaved from running away. By 1851, Cartwright became professor of diseases of the negro at the University of Louisiana and was deemed an expert on Black behavior. That year, he published a paper titled "Report on the Diseases and Physical Peculiarities of the Negro Race," which appeared in *The New Orleans Medical and Surgical Journal,* a reputable scholarly publication of the time.[2]

Cartwright's theories were readily accepted because the law had already begun to link radicalized slaves who were "disobedient" to mental illness. Cartwright compared fugitive slaves to fugitive cats, who left their owners only in bouts of joy before coming back.[3] Claims that runaway slaves were mentally ill also had benefits for slaveowners. Because enslaved men and women were also considered commodities, if a slave buyer could prove a slave had a mental health condition and the previous owner knew of this illness, the buyer could get his money back.[4] This was known as redhibition, a civil law claim brought against a product's seller and/or manufacturer. The buyer would seek a full refund or a reduction in the purchase price due to a hidden defect that prevented the product from performing the task for which it was purchased.[5]

Another disease was "dysaesthesia aethiopica," which was an "illness" Cartwright and other prominent physicians claimed caused laziness in slaves.[6] According to Dr. Cartwright's "Diseases and Peculiarities of the Negro Race:" "They wander about at night, and keep in a half nodding sleep during the day. They slight their work— cut up corn, cane, cotton, or tobacco when hoeing it, as if for pure mischief. They raise disturbances with their overseers and fellow-servants without cause or motive, and seem to be insensible to pain when subjected to punishment."[7]

Understanding mental illness and its role in the enslavement and oppression of Black people is essential because it offers a window into how pro-slavery advocates justified slavery as a way to perpetuate it. Consider the story of the white overseer who used mental illness to explain away why he had killed an enslaved man named Samuel.[8]

According to the story, the overseer got word that Samuel had become unmanageable, that he was destroying cotton, and that even after being ordered to be whipped, Samuel said he would not be whipped. Both of Samuel's acts—his destruction of the cotton crop and his unwillingness to submit to whipping—represented symptoms for what Cartwright deemed "dysaesthesia aethiopica," and thus, the murder was justified.[9]

From James Marion Sims, who experimented on Black women's bodies without anesthesia[10] to Ota Benga and Saartjie Baartman, whose bodies were displayed like animals, the medical and scientific field has an extensive history of racism against African Americans. Consider that Blacks were often wrongfully admitted to mental institutions. Studies conducted in 1973 in the *Archives of General Psychiatry* showed that African American patients were more likely to be diagnosed as schizophrenic than white patients.[11]

Beyond mental health, medical professionals and slave owners also worked together in mistreating and abusing Black people's cells.

Rebecca Skloot's book, *The Immortal Life of Henrietta Lacks,* and Oprah Winfrey's film adaptation brought attention to the widespread illegal use of the HeLa cell line.[12] The scientific name for HeLa is Helacyton Gartleri,[13] and they were the first line of human cells to survive in vitro (in a test tube).

The cells came from a Black woman named Henrietta Lacks. Ms. Lacks went to Johns Hopkins on February 1, 1951, due to a severe knot in her cervix and bloody discharge.[14] She was identified as having cervical cancer after a biopsy.[15] At the time, The Johns Hopkins Hospital was one of only a few hospitals to treat poor African Americans. Prior to the therapy, cells from the tumor were taken for research without Lack's knowledge or consent, as was customary at the time.[16] Henrietta underwent radium treatments, and a sample of her cells were taken, and a biopsy was sent to Dr. George Gey who cultivated another sample, again without Lack's knowledge or consent, in a subsequent round. He quickly realized HeLa cells were different from other cells. While the others died, these kept growing.

After more than fifty years, there are billions of HeLa cells in laboratories worldwide. It is the most used cell line, and it is known to be extremely resilient.

Two scientists, Dr. Russell W. Brown and James H. M. Henderson, made their mark by leading a team of researchers and staff at Tuskegee University in the mass production of the HeLa cells for the development of the polio vaccine.[17] Scientists of the time believed that Blacks were immune to the virus, which led to the disregard for the suffering of Black Americans with the disease.[18]

# CHAPTER EIGHT

## What You Didn't Learn about Uncle Tom

S tereotypes about African Americans have been around since slavery and emerged from minstrel shows. Also called minstrelsy, these theatrical stage performances were popular from the early nineteenth to the early twentieth century.[1] The earliest shows were of white men who mocked the singing and dancing of enslaved people with their faces painted black. They used burnt cork, painted grotesquely exaggerated white mouths over their own (sometimes wearing bright red lipstick), and wore woolly black wigs. The character they created was Jim Crow.[2]

The most misunderstood and controversial stereotype is the Uncle Tom.

When Harriet Beecher Stowe published *Uncle Tom's Cabin* in 1852, it galvanized public opinion. The book sold 10,000 copies in the first week and 300,000 in its first year.[3] What we didn't learn about Uncle Tom is that Harriet Beecher Stowe based her character on the life of a Black man named Josiah Henson.

Author, abolitionist, and minister, Henson escaped slavery in 1830 with his wife and children and found refuge in Canada. In 1841, he started a freeman settlement called the British American Institute, which became known as one of the final stops on the Underground Railroad.[4] Henson went back to free people, helping 118 slaves escape. Josiah Henson also developed a sawmill producing high-quality black lumber that won him a medal at the first World's Fair in London. He also maintained a farm, raised horses, and bred them.

Henson helped hundreds of enslaved men, women, and children escape North years before the Underground Railroad. He was a good man and a great leader.[5]

So how did he become associated with such a negative connotation?

While Stowe's character forced people to see the humanity in enslaved Black people, some also saw Tom as *extra* kind to white slaveholders. This led to the use of the term "Uncle Tom" (or shortened to Tom) as a derogatory word to describe a subservient Black person or "house negro."[5] Malcolm X described the connotation of the house negro in this way, "...whenever that house Negro identified himself, he always identified himself in the same sense that his master identified himself. When his master said, 'We have good food,' the house Negro would say, 'Yes, we have plenty of good food.' 'we' have plenty of good food. When the master said that 'We have a fine home here,' the house Negro said, 'Yes, we have a fine home here.' When the master would be sick, the house Negro identified himself so much with his master he'd say, 'What's the matter boss, we sick?' His master's pain was his pain."[6]

The Tom represented a smiling, dark-skinned servant always ready and willing to please. His symbols are the following: the dependable worker, the maid, mammy, butler, porter, or waiter. Unlike the buck, who was obstinate and couldn't be broken, Tom was easy to work with, did not question authority, and even defended the enslaver before his own people.[7]

Occasionally, the master would give Tom privileges to deceive him into thinking he was set apart from the other enslaved men and women: a bit more to eat, a spot in the attic of the big house, or maybe even his own little shack. However, despite Tom's loyalty, he was still beaten, sold, cursed, slapped, kicked, flogged, and worked as a horse like the others.

The term "Uncle Tom" reflected the era. Regardless of their age, all Black men were called by their first names or referred to as "boy," "uncle," and "old man." If the white person did not know a Black person personally, the term "nigger" or "nigger-fellow" could be used. In court and the press, Blacks were frequently referred to as "negros" with a first name, such as "Negro Sam."[8] The term "Jack" or some other common name was also used to address Black men who were unknown to the white speaker.[9]

Whites portrayed the Tom as old, physically weak, and psychologically dependent on whites for approval; for this, he was not just a Tom but an *Uncle* Tom. The "uncle" part was intended to strip him of his authority. An enslaved man was not a man, and enslavers did not address him as a man. Titles like mister did not exist for him. Instead, he was an *uncle* or a *boy*.

Similar actions were taken toward Black women who were not referred to as Miss or Mrs., but *auntie* or *girl/gal*.

Josiah Henson became a leader in a growing number of fugitive slaves in Canada. He was also the driving force behind the Dawn Settlement in Dresden, Ontario, to employ and educate formerly enslaved people.[10]

Harriet Beecher Stowe was angered when the Fugitive Slave Act was established in 1850, requiring enslaved people to be returned to their masters regardless of whether they were in a free state and granting the US government permission to track down and recapture fugitive slaves.[11] She decided to write a book to combat that influence. She read slave narratives and eventually came across Josiah Henson.

However, over time, Henson's legacy would fade from memory as Stowe's fictional character would become the symbol for *any* Black person who exemplified an inkling of dignity. No longer was Uncle Tom the subservient Black person psychologically dependent on whites for approval. *Now*, Uncle Tom would be used as a derogatory term for a*ny* Black person who showed intelligence, refinement, and pride. However, this characteristic is more akin to being a Sambo, not an Uncle Tom.

When Black people refer to other Black people as Uncle Tom, they are saying that person likes to please white people, acts like white people, or is weak and docile when it comes to white people.

## The Sambo

The Sambo was portrayed as a lazy, easily frightened, chronically idle, and inarticulate buffoon. Sambo was depicted as a perpetual child incapable of living as an independent adult. The core of the Sambo caricature was his constant happiness. White actors depicted him as bug-eyed, with a wide-toothed smile and exaggerated facial features, like giant lips. Literature also played a significant role in perpetuating stereotypes, like *Little Black Sambo*, published in 1899 by Scotswoman, Helen Bannerman. The book is about a little boy who takes his clothes off piece by piece, which ferocious tigers fight over. The tigers run so fast that they turn into butter. Sambo's father scoops the pool of butter up on his way home, and Sambo's mother uses it to make a pancake feast for dinner.[12]

The Sambo could also be used interchangeably with the coon.

## The Coon

The coon (from the word racoon) was considered an adult who acted like a child. Racist whites did not want to portray African Americans as human beings who read, wrote, or displayed any characteristics of intelligence, esteem, or professionalism. They wanted to picture Black people as ignorant, foolish, stupid, and childish because it justified slavery.

Lincoln Theodore Monroe Andrew Perry is the prototype for the sambo/coon stereotype. Known by his stage name as Stepin Fetchit, his signature was that he was the world's laziest man. Perry's characteristics were always sleepy, with teary eyes and slow speech. He took minutes to complete simple sentences. A scene of him lying in bed in pajamas taking three whole minutes to answer the phone and then another entire minute to say "hello" (as in "Lazy Richard")[13] is what viewers could expect of his stage performances. "Perry epitomized the mumbling, shuffling, buck-eyed buffoon who acted like he didn't know his ass from a hole in the ground."[14] Stepin Fetchit became one of the top paid Black entertainers of his time while manifesting the coon. Perry's role as a lazy Black man came served as a universal symbol that all Black people were idle. It was as if being well-spoken was a white trait that African Americans had no right to possess.

While Harriet Beecher Stowe's bestseller was meant to rally the moral sentiments of whites against the horrors of slavery, Uncle Tom's Cabin also ironically reinforced racial stereotypes. An enslaved man named Sam (Uncle Tom's first owner) offered much comic relief in the book, and was clearly modeled after the Coon with traces of the Sambo.[15] Another character, an enslaved man named Adolph on St. Clare's plantation (who wears his master's old clothes), acts like a Coon.[16] It's hard to tell if Stowe purposely exploited these stereotypes to appeal to northern whites (who would already be familiar with and adore them from minstrel shows) or if she thought they were accurately indicative of Black people.

What we know is that while the book sparked much support for the anti-slavery movement, it also simultaneously made life worse for many African Americans by perpetuating racial stereotypes.[17] White southerners also attacked Stowe and her book for showcasing Blacks as fully human.[18] One political cartoon depicted her in hell, surrounded by demons and holding a book titled *Uncle Tom's Cabin: I Love the Blacks*.[19] Additionally, in response to the book were novels presenting slavery as a wonderful institution sanctioned by the bible and the laws of the land.[20]

Thus, we no longer remember the man from whom the character was inspired, the great lengths Josiah Henson went to free his people, and how he displayed qualities that were anything but those associated with that of the Sambo or sell-out. Not only was Josiah Henson no buffoon, but also neither are most Black men and women we refer to as "Toms." Instead, they are often well-spoken and educated (like Henson), precisely the qualities the enslaver did not want those they enslaved to exemplify.

# CHAPTER NINE

## What You Didn't Learn about Convict Leasing

With nearly half of all cotton investments in human bodies now gone, the end of chattel slavery left a sour taste in the mouths of enslavers. Over four million African Americans were poured into a society that did not want them, cotton economies were in shambles, cotton gins were destroyed, and wealth deteriorated before the ink could dry on the Emancipation Proclamation. Whites mourned over the loss of riches, the suffering of the war, and the humiliation of Union soldiers camped out in their towns.[1] But nothing compared to whites' fear that the formerly enslaved would rule governments and take their masters' lands. A system so interwoven into the fabric of America could not just be taken away without severe consequences. Enslavers refused to sit back and watch. A reconstruction of slavery was necessary.

The Freedmen's Bureau was established in 1865 by Congress to provide aid in food, housing, medical care, and education to formerly enslaved Blacks.[2] However, President Abraham Lincoln was shot five days after the war on April 15, 1865, at Ford's Theatre in Washington, D. C. and Vice President Andrew Johnson assumed the presidency.[3] Johnson rescinded these provisions a few months later, and African Americans remained the property of landowners, working on the same plantations that held them as enslaved people. All of this was despite General William T. Sherman's plan to grant freedmen forty acres on the islands and the coastal region of Georgia. After the Civil War, African Americans never received their forty acres. They were ordered to either sign contracts with the owners or be evicted and driven out by army troops. In 1865, the government ordered all land to be returned to its original owners. The result was that millions of Blacks remained poor.[4]

In the 1890s, southern states enacted a new form of black codes called Jim Crow laws. These laws made it illegal for Blacks and whites to share public facilities. Black codes and Jim Crow laws were born out of the slave codes of chattel slavery, a set of rules based on the concept that African Americans were property, not people.[5] As the US government abolished slavery, they also devised plans to restructure it, remixing these rules so that they could continue to rule over African Americans as masters. One way enslavers kept Blacks, specifically Black men, in captivity was through a subtle, but powerful loophole in the 13th Amendment,[6] that allowed slavery as punishment for a crime which gave birth to such injustices as the system of convict leasing.[7] New laws targeted Blacks, criminalizing their lives. Almost everything African Americans did was a crime, from farm owners who were incapable of walking by the railroad or selling the products of their farm after dark to the infamous Pig Laws, where stealing a pig (or any animal) could result in five years imprisonment.[8]

Convict leasing began in Alabama in 1846 until July 1, 1928. In 1883, about 10 percent of Alabama's total revenue came from convict leasing.[9] In 1898, nearly 73 percent of total revenue came from this same source. Death rates among leased convicts were ten times higher than the death rates of prisoners in non-lease states. In 1873, for example, 25 percent of all Black leased convicts died.[10]

The more African Americans broke these laws and were sentenced to prison, the more enslaved people the plantation owners (now masked under private parties and corporations) symbolically and politically had back in their possession. They could work the prisoners from sunup to sundown, while providing them with food, clothing, and shelter. Under the system of convict leasing—the leasing of bodies to coal and iron companies owned by former enslavers—slavery was back.[11]

## Attica State Prison

With awareness growing out of the civil rights movement of the 1960s, Malcolm X, and the Black Panther Party, Black and Latino prisoners of 1970 began organizing rebellions against their treatment within the prison system. The rebellions spread from prison-to-prison until they came to a head on the Thursday morning of September 9, 1971. When the door prisoners used to go to the yard was locked, a fight broke out between the guards. As the fight grew, more prisoners joined until they broke open a gate connecting to another part of the institution, and prisoners were let loose.

The brothers locked the prison down, taking staff members as hostages and implementing their own order system.[12] Appointing leaders to keep order and ensure the staff was properly cared for, they demanded better treatment within the prison system from the outside world. An example of their demands was better medical treatment and less slave labor.[13] However, the prisoners' "freedom" would not last long. When a hostage hit in the head at the beginning of the fight died from his injuries, the prisoners were responsible under the felony-murder rule. The felony was the riot, and the murder was the guard's death.[14]

Shortly after, a National Guard helicopter flew low over the yard and blew a cloud of military-grade CS gas into the crowd of men. Frank "Big Black" Smith, one of the surviving prisoners of the time,[15] recalled the following, as told to attorney Jefferey Haas: "First came the tear gas. People looked for something to cover their face. When I first heard the shots, I thought they were blanks. Then the people around me in the yard started dropping. I realized they were real bullets, and everyone ducked and ran for cover."[16]

The gunshots Frank referred to were the marksmen who came in and started shooting, hitting 189 of the 1300 men in the yard and killing thirty-one people—twenty-nine prisoners and ten hostages. There is a conflict between the numbers. After the shooting, Frank said, "The guards stripped us naked after the shooting. They made us crawl naked in the mud through a gauntlet where they beat us."[17] Next, Frank was tortured as an example. They burned his body with cigarettes.[18]

Later, a news photographer discovered and captured two inscriptions scribbled with white markers in separate hands on a dark steel wall that summarized the history of the Attica uprising.[19]

"Attica fell 9-9-71 - F*&k you pig!"

Just underneath that was written,

"Retaken 9-13-71.

31 Dead Niggers."

While seeking freedom, the men had forgotten one thing: slavery was abolished *except as a punishment for a crime.* They gave these Black men slave-like treatment because they had been re-enslaved as prisoners of the law.

# CHAPTER TEN

## What You Didn't Learn about Slave Patrols

There were two types of policing in the early colonies. The "Watch" or private-for-profit policing, which is referred to as "The Big Stick," was both informal and communal.[1] The watch system were groups of community volunteers whose job was to warn people of impending danger.

Next to the watchmen was a system of constables. Constables were official law enforcement officers who had a variety of non-law enforcement functions to perform, including supervising the activities of the night watch.[2]

In the American South, policing has its roots in another system: the slave patrol.

Slave patrols had three functions: to chase, apprehend, and return the enslaved who had run away to their "owners," organize terror to deter slave revolts, and maintain discipline for "slave-workers" who were subject to violence if they broke plantation rules.[3] These organizations evolved into southern police departments to control the formerly enslaved people working as laborers and to enforce the Jim Crow segregation laws that denied freed people certain human rights.[4]

Slave patrollers were white men who rode around on horseback carrying guns, rope, and whips, ready to capture the enslaved. Their job was to enforce the pass system, a pass or ticket signed by the enslaver that authorized the enslaved to travel.[5] Without this pass, a slave patroller could beat an enslaved person, and beatings sometimes happened even when they had a pass,[6] eerily similar to Black men and women who are beaten, choked, gunned down, and stepped on by police even when they have done nothing wrong. Slave patrols used to be so commonplace that there was a song describing it that Blacks used to sing, "run, nigger, run; the pateroller catch you."[7]

> Early American police departments shared two primary characteristics: they were notoriously corrupt and flagrantly brutal. This should come as no surprise in that police were under the control of local politicians. The local political party ward leader in most cities appointed the police executive in charge of the ward leader's neighborhood. The ward leader, also, most often was the neighborhood tavern

owner, sometimes the neighborhood purveyor of gambling and prostitution, and usually the controlling influence over neighborhood youth gangs who were used to get out the vote and intimidate opposition party voters. In this system of vice, organized violence, and political corruption, it is inconceivable that the police could be anything but corrupt. (Dr. Gary Potter, July 2, 2013)[8]

There is evidence that, prior to the American Civil War, a legally recognized law enforcement system existed in the country with the specific aim of managing the slave population and defending the rights of slave owners.[9] Furthermore, groups of men on horseback at night, could terrify slaves into submission.[10] Consequently, the practice of slave patrols has maintained its terror. Many members of the Black community still refer to large police vehicles as "pattywagons," a play on the former "paddy rollers," which was also a nickname for slave patrols.[11] The parallels between the slave patrols and contemporary American policing are simply too obvious to ignore or reject. Thus, it is appropriate to view the slave patrol as a precursor of contemporary American law enforcement.[12]

During Jim Crow, it was unlawful for Black people to be treated with the same respect as white people. As a result, part of enforcing the law meant treating Blacks inhumanely, excluding them from sitting at lunch counters or drinking from water fountains reserved for whites only. It was lawful to lynch a Black man for speaking to, lying with, or even looking at a white woman, as was the case of William "Froggie" James (see Chapter 1).

When the US justice system is designed to enforce the law, what happens when people organize the laws in ways that discriminate against Black people? What happens when the "crimes" being prevented are Black people rebelling against unjust systems of oppression? What happens when the criminals being apprehended are disproportionally Black? What happens when they are run down, captured, and gunned down even when they are *not* breaking the law, just like the slave patrollers did to the freedmen?

Arrested and tried for the murder of Trayvon Martin in Sanford, Florida, on February 26, 2012, George Zimmerman was acquitted of all charges in *Florida v. George Zimmerman* on July 13, 2013.

On February 23, 2020, three white men (Travis McMichael, Travis's father, Gregory McMichael, and William "Roddie" Bryan) murdered Ahmaud Arbery, a twenty-five-year-old Black man who was killed while jogging through a Georgia neighborhood, sparking a nationwide outcry. The men were arrested in May 2020 and faced nine charges, including murder and aggravated assault.[13]

Gregory McMichael told police he thought Arbery looked like a suspect in a series of break-ins, though no reported break-ins had been filed.[14] McMichael and his son armed themselves with a pistol and a shotgun and pursued Arbery with a pick-up truck, where they fired three shots, killing Arbery.[15] According to an article on the British Broadcasting Corporation's (BBC) website, all three men said "Stop, stop, we want to talk to you."[16] Three shots were fired, and Arbery fell down on the street. A post-mortem examination showed Arbery had two gunshot wounds in his chest, and a gunshot graze wound on the inside of one of his wrists. He did not have drugs or alcohol in his system.[17]

The McMichaels were given life sentences without the possibility of parole plus twenty years on January 7, 2022, while Bryan received a life sentence with the possibility of parole after thirty years. The three guys were convicted in a federal court on February 22, 2022, of attempted kidnapping and hate crime.

Just three months after Arbery's death, on May 25, 2020, a policeman killed George Floyd, another unarmed Black man. Floyd's murder sparked global outrage, protests, and unrest. Images and footage of the officer, Derek Chauvin—who had eighteen prior complaints against him according to the Minneapolis Police Department's Internal Affairs[18]—kneeling on Floyd's neck as he repeated the now familiar phrase, "I can't breathe!" was horrifying, heartbreaking, and looked like something out of 1960's Alabama.[19]

In response to the looting that occurred after Floyd's death, former US President Donald Trump called the looters "thugs," commenting that "when the looting starts, the shooting starts."[20] The phrase is derived from a 1967 quote used by Miami's police chief, Walter Headley, when he addressed his department's "crackdown on...slum hoodlums."[21]

From the 1965 Watts Riots that broke out over Marquette Frye, to the police officers who beat Rodney King in 1991 and the riots that broke out over their acquittal in 1992, US practices of policing when it comes to the African American community are eerily similar to the activities of the southern slave patroller.

# CHAPTER ELEVEN

## What You Didn't Learn about the *State of Missouri v Celia*

The first elected legislature in the colonies, the Virginia House of Burgesses, convened to discuss whether or not enslaved children should follow the English tradition of having their status follow their father or if they should follow their mother.[1] Fearful that enslaved children of mixed ancestry would benefit significantly from the freedom of their white fathers, colonist decided that "all children borne in this country shall be held bond or free only according to the condition of the mother."[2] This showed the long-lasting tradition that when white women produced children, their status in society followed the man, but when Black women had children, their offspring were treated as property.[3]

Adopted from the Roman principle of partus sequitur ventrem—"the offspring follows the belly"—used to determine the ownership of animals—this opened the door for white men to profit from their sexual assault of Black women.[4] Enslavers now had the legal right to rape enslaved women while increasing their wealth.[5] Evidence of this *privilege* of the Black woman's body can be seen clearly in the case of an enslaved girl named Celia, who, on the night of June 23, 1855, took a club to her abuser's head and killed him.[6]

Around 1820, Robert Newsom and his family left Virginia and headed west, settling land along the Middle River in southern Callaway County, Missouri. In 1849, Newsom's wife died, and in the summer of 1850, he purchased a sixth enslaved person from an enslaver in neighboring Audrain County, a fourteen-year-old girl named Celia.[7]

Newsome owned 800 acres of land and livestock, including horses, milk cows, beef cattle, hogs, sheep, and two oxen. Like most Callaway County farmers, Newsom also enslaved people—five male slaves. He bought Celia specifically to have sex with her, raping her for the first time on the way home from the sale. Robert kept her locked away in a tiny cabin on his farm (located in a grove of fruit trees some distance from his main house) and raped her repeatedly for five years.[8]

One day, Celia decided it would be the last time he forced himself on her. In the fifth year, Celia ran to a cabin corner when Newsom told her it was time for sex. He moved closer to her. Then Celia took a stick left there earlier in the day, raised it, and smacked Newsome hard in the head. He dropped to the floor, and Celia struck him again, killing him.[9]

After killing Newsom, Celia burned his body in her fireplace all night. The search team discovered Newsom's ashes next to the path leading to the stables after Celia made her confession. Additionally, they collected bone fragments from Celia's fireplace, larger bone pieces from beneath the hearthstone, as well as Newsom's burned buckle, buttons, and charcoal pocketknife. The collected objects were put in a box to be displayed during the next inquest.[10]

In 1854, Missouri law provided that any woman could defend herself against anyone who forcefully assaulted her. However, this law did not apply to Celia. The court ruled that she did not fall under the category of *any woman* as an enslaved woman and was guilty of murder in the first degree. The night before her death, Celia was questioned one last time in her cell. Once more, she vehemently denied that anyone helped or encouraged her in any way. She told her interrogator, as reported in the *Fulton Telegraph*, "as soon as I struck him the Devil got into me, and I struck him with a stick until he was dead, and then rolled him into the fire and burnt him up."[11]

After giving birth to a stillborn child, Celia died by hanging at 2:30 P.M. on December 21, 1855.[12]

The law of *partus sequitur ventrem* also opened the door for Black women to be raped by *any* man, Black or white, since courts did not recognize the rape of enslaved women and girls as a crime.[13] Black women had no right to protect themselves against forced sex because they had no right to refuse sex to white slaveowners.[14]

In the 1850s, an enslaved man named George was convicted of raping a ten-year-old girl. John D. Freeman, the lawyer representing George, argued that because the law does not recognize enslaved people's marital or sexual rights, the crime of rape did not exist between African slaves. The courts agreed and threw out the indictment.[15]

These laws illustrated what Malcolm X said: "The most disrespected person in America is the Black woman. The most unprotected person in America is the Black woman. The most neglected person in America is the Black woman." [16]

# CHAPTER TWELVE

## What You Didn't Learn about Abraham Lincoln's Colonization Plan

"Honest Abe," the "Rail-Splitter," and the "Great Emancipator" are a few names used to describe America's sixteenth president. Born on February 12, 1809, near Hodgenville, Kentucky, Abraham Lincoln is most famous for preserving the Union during the American Civil War and bringing about the emancipation of enslaved people in the United States.[1]

However, on freeing the slaves, Lincoln once stated that even if he could acknowledge that freeing the enslaved would make Black people politically and socially equal to white people, it is not something the mass of white people would admit.[2] Therefore, before he wrote the Emancipation Proclamation, several efforts were made to preserve the Union *without* freeing the enslaved. These efforts included colonization, or the idea that much of the African American population should leave the United States and settle in Africa or Central America.

On August 14, 1862, five years after The Dred Scott Decision[3] that reiterated Blacks were not, and as "a second class of persons,"[4] *could not* be citizens, Abraham Lincoln hosted a "Deputation of Free Negroes"[5] event at the White House. Led by the Rev. Joseph Mitchell, commissioner of emigration for the Interior Department, it was the first time African Americans had been invited to the White House to weigh in on a political matter.

Lincoln planned to produce a document that would not only free the enslaved but, once freed, call on them to leave the country voluntarily, saying, "I think your race suffer very greatly, many of them by living among us, while ours suffer from your presence."[6]

This idea, colonization, was not new but had been circulating among white racists, elites, and eugenicists since the 1700s. The American Colonization Society (ACS) was founded in 1816 in Washington, D.C., by white politicians and enslavers who wanted to encourage free Blacks to leave the country and live in West Africa.[7] ACS and its many chapters hoped this would rid them of free Black people while preserving slavery.

According to Rick Beard, New York Times writer of "Lincoln's Panama Plan," the ACS had very little success; between 1816 and 1860, the group transported roughly 11,000 Black people to Africa, most emancipated. In contrast, up to 20,000 African Americans voluntarily emigrated during the American Revolution, and many more made their way to Canada via the Underground Railroad in the first half of the nineteenth century.[8]

Organizations, such as the ACS, not only spoke on colonization, but also the US government allocated much money for its implementation. In April 1862, Congress passed the District of Columbia Act, emancipating enslaved persons in Washington and appropriating $100,000 to resettle "such free persons of African descent now residing in said District, including those liberated by this act, as may desire to emigrate."[9] Congress also spent an additional $500,000 to colonize enslaved persons whose enslavers were disloyal to the United States.[10] On July 16, 1861, the House Select Committee on Emancipation and Colonization recommended twenty million dollars for settling confiscated enslaved people beyond United States' borders. All of this is in addition to a government-funded $600,000 to ship free Black people to another country.[11]

Lincoln's belief in the benefits of colonization was unaffected by the opposition. Ambrose W. Thompson, the leader of the Chiriqu Improvement Society, and the new president had their first meeting on April 10, 1861, two days before Fort Sumter was bombarded. During this discussion, it was decided to look into the idea of starting an immigrant colony in Panama where recently freed slaves could work as coal miners for the Navy.[12]

The first version of Emancipation advocated for colonization, and in an annual address to Congress, Lincoln called for a constitutional amendment that would aid in this plan.[13] Eric Foner wrote, according to Beard, that "colonization represented a middle ground between the radicalism of the abolitionists and the prospect of the United States' existing permanently half slave and half free."[14] However, this was Lincoln's last known public mention of colonization from which Frederick Douglass called "a safety valve...for white racism," and that the meeting showed "a desire to get rid of Black Americans."[15]

As the war progressed, policymakers faced pressure to develop strategies to manage the growing number of enslaved people who fled Union lines. They had to do something. Thus, Lincoln issued the Emancipation Proclamation on January 1, 1863, to preserve the Union, ending slavery in the States in Rebellion, meaning that this decree did not free all enslaved people.[16] It excluded slavery from the border states of Maryland, Delaware, Kentucky, and Missouri but included slavery in the Union-occupied sections of Tennessee, Virginia, and Louisiana.[17]

Furthermore, Lincoln clearly expressed his opinion when he wrote the following: "My paramount object in this struggle is to save the Union, and is not either to save or destroy Slavery. If I could save the Union without freeing any slave, I would do it, and if I could save it by freeing all the slaves, I would do it, and if I could save it by freeing some and leaving others alone, I would also do that. What I do about Slavery and the colored race, I do because I believe it helps to save this Union."[18]

On the passing of the 13th Amendment in January of 1865, slavery was officially deemed illegal in America. However, it did not free all enslaved persons. In Texas, men, women, and children were still being held in bondage and did not know that slavery had ended. Due to this, slaveowners in surrounding states steadily moved themselves and their slaves to Texas in an attempt to flee the idea of freedom.[19]

These men, women, and children were still enslaved until June 19, 1865. Major General Gordon Granger led Union soldiers, who landed at Galveston, Texas, with news that the war had ended. The enslaved were now free two-and-a-half years after President Lincoln's Emancipation Proclamation. It is the reason many Black Americans celebrate what is called Juneteenth (combining the month of June and the 19th) instead of July 4th as their National Independence Day.[20]

Abraham Lincoln was assassinated on April 15, 1865, making Andrew Johnson president. By December 1865, Johnson offered pardons to former slaveowners, which authorized them to create new state governments. The people who led Johnson's Reconstruction are the same ones who led the Confederacy, who were also former enslavers. Immediately after African Americans in Texas were freed from chattel slavery in June of 1865, they were required to have labor contracts, and many Blacks returned to their former slaveowners.[21]

One method by which slavery persisted after the Civil War was convict leasing (see Chapter 9). By now we know how prisoners worked in cruel, hazardous, and frequently fatal conditions while states made money.[22] Up to the 1930s, thousands of Black people were coerced into what Douglas A. Blackmon referred to as "slavery by another name."[23]

Although physically freed, African Americans were held economically, emotionally, psychologically, and spiritually captive in the United States for over 400 years. Black people in the United States have been held captive to almost one hundred years of Jim Crow Laws, over eighty years of lynchings, fourteen years of fighting for civil rights, and countless years of police brutality that persists to this day.

The promises made to freedmen at the abolition of slavery were never realized because perhaps, as Lincoln put it, the purpose was never to free them in the first place but to save the Union. Once the United States reestablished the Union, America essentially recreated slavery through laws and legislation that severely limited the citizenship rights of Black people.

Promises such as owning land were broken when Johnson ordered nearly all land in the hands of the government to be returned to its pre-war owners—slave/plantation owners.

The Emancipation Proclamation, Reconstruction, and Juneteenth did nothing to restore land or citizenship rights to the forty million newly freed Blacks. Instead, Black people have remained psychologically and economically disadvantaged, forced into mental and spiritual enslavement that has lasted for centuries.

# CHAPTER THIRTEEN

## What You Didn't Learn about Black History Month

Today, Black History Month is celebrated by all people who wish to acknowledge the plight and sacrifices of Black Americans. Dr. Carter G. Woodson's contributions have become something of a holiday in the Black community.

In the summer of 1915, Dr. Carter G. Woodson, an alumnus of the University of Chicago, traveled from Washington, D. C. to participate in a national celebration of the fiftieth anniversary of emancipation sponsored by the state of Illinois. Three years later, Woodson joined the exhibitions with his Black history display and later decided to form an organization to promote the scientific study of Black life and history. Dr. Woodson said, "If a race has no history, it has no worth-while tradition, it becomes a negligible factor in the thought of the world, and it stands in danger of being exterminated."[1]

The Association for the Study of Negro Life and History, which eventually changed its name to the Association for the Study of Afro-American Life and History, was founded on September 9 of that year when Woodson and three other individuals convened at the Wabash YMCA. Woodson would carry on his tradition of ground-breaking accomplishments by founding the African American-owned Associated Publishers Press in 1921 and the Journal of Negro History in 1916. His intention was to put African Americans' accomplishments front and center.[2] Dr. Carter G. Woodson went on to write a dozen books, including *A Century of Negro Migration* (1918), *The History of the Negro Church* (1921), *The Negro in Our History* (1922), and (one of his most famous books to date), *The Mis-Education of the Negro* (1933).

In 1924, Dr. Woodson's work contributed to the creation of Negro History and Literature Week, which was renamed Negro Achievement Week. This weeklong celebration eventually became Negro History Month and then Black History Month.

But Black History Month couldn't have been created without the help of the nation's young people.

Students have always been at the forefront of change. It was students who left their classrooms during the civil rights movement to march in the streets for equality. It was kids who were being bitten by dogs and sprayed with water hoses. Thus, it is no surprise that it was also young people who helped Black History Month become a monthlong celebration. "The first people to celebrate Black History Month were the Black students and educators at Kent State University."[3] These students celebrated during January and February. It only made sense to follow their lead and make it official.

While Dr. Carter G. Woodson is known as the father of Black History Month, and Black youth popularized the celebration, they still needed help with funding. In 1916, Woodson borrowed $400 against his $2,000 life insurance policy to publish the first issue of the *Journal of Negro Life and History*.[4] Woodson received this financial help from three powerful organizations that would heavily influence the culture, the Carnegie Foundation, The Rockefeller Foundation, and the Rosenwald Foundation (now known as the Rosenwald Fund).[5] Woodson's proposals to these organizations were rejected for many years and he struggled to support himself, the association, and the journal.

Finally, the Carnegie Institute awarded Woodson his first grant of $25,000. Unfortunately, while these groups eventually gave Dr. Woodson the funding he needed to succeed, the discriminatory role these same organizations played in their treatment of African Americans should not be overlooked.

One of the most infamous examples is the Tuskegee experiment. In conjunction with the Public Health Service (PHS), the Rosenwald Fund, headed by a Jewish immigrant who helped build the Sears and Roebuck Company into a giant mail-order business,[6] sponsored a syphilis seroprevalence pilot program in 1929. This pilot program would become widely known as "The Tuskegee Syphilis Experiment," in which syphilis was intentionally left untreated in adult Black men in the South. It was initially called "Tuskegee Study of Untreated Syphilis in the Negro Male" (now referred to as the "SPHS Syphilis Study at Tuskegee").[7] The Rosenwald Fund and PHS collaborated to fund the "SPHS Syphilis Study at Tuskegee" to integrate health programs for southern Blacks.[8] As a result, in November 1929, the trustees voted to spend up to $50,000 during the 1930 calendar year.[9]

The study was successful due to the perception that syphilis was widespread in the Black community due to "high libido" and "widespread sexual promiscuity."[10] Consequently, the study involved 600 Black men—200 who did not have syphilis.[10] Furthermore, Black men were lured into participating with promises of rides to and from their appointments and stipends paid to the survivors of the men who died.[11]

In the 1997 film *Miss Evers Boys,* starring Alfre Woodard (whose character is loosely based on Nurse Eunice Rivers, the Black woman who trained at Tuskegee University),[12] researchers told participants they were being treated for "bad blood." This was a term used by southern Blacks of the time to describe several ailments. Using this colloquial phrase posed a problem because Black people referred to many ailments as "bad blood," which left them with a lack of understanding about what syphilis was. Sadly, many were unaware. Physicians used the terms interchangeably. This confused the people with other ailments that needed attention. "A number of cases which had received reports that their blood was all right insisted they were not all right."[13] One woman thought the "government shots" were causing people to have babies. "Them shots is making them babies," she said. "You reckon them shots make you have babies? I sho' don't want no more and if they do, I rather have bad blood."[14]

Contrary to popular belief, this experiment was not about whether the Black men had syphilis. Macon County was the poorest of the six counties with the highest syphilis rate–approximately 40%. Macon's medical facilities for rural Blacks were also meager.[15] In addition, the cost of medical care included a mileage fee for home visits and an examination fee.[16] People whose incomes were less than one dollar could not afford health care, resulting in many diseases and illnesses among those who either refused to go to the doctor or could not afford it.

The SPHS Syphilis Study at Tuskegee was about how the disease would perform if left untreated. These poor Black men did not know they were volunteering to die.

By 1943, penicillin was the treatment of choice for syphilis. However, doctors did not give the men anything that would help cure them of the disease. Instead, these men were told to apply a mercury ointment to their abdomen every morning and then tie a belt around the area all day.[17] Not only were these men being experimented on until their deaths, but also they were being humiliated and mocked.[18]

The **SPHS** Syphilis Study at Tuskegee did not officially end until October 1972. An official apology wasn't issued until May 16, 1997, twenty-five years later.[19]

Nevertheless, this is not the first time the Rosenwald Fund was involved in the affairs of Black lives.

From the 1910s through the 1930s, the Julius Rosenwald Fund was a significant force in North Carolina education. Its matching grants aided in constructing more than 800 public school buildings for African American children. In addition to helping to fund Black History Month and southern schools, the Rosenwald Fund is also responsible for funding Black movements such as the Harlem Renaissance.

Focused on redefining what it meant to be Black by forging a new identity, the new negro movement as it was first called, was a cultural revival of Black music, dance, art, fashion, literature, theater, and politics centered in Harlem during the 1920s and 1930s. It produced such talents as W. E. B. Du Bois, Josephine Baker, and Paul Robeson; writers and poets Zora Neale Hurston, Effie Lee Newsome, and Countee Cullen; visual artists Aaron Douglas and Augusta Savage; and an impressive list of legendary musicians, including Louis Armstrong, Count Basie, Eubie Blake, Cab Calloway, Duke Ellington, Billie Holiday, Ivie Anderson, Fats Waller, Jelly Roll Morton, and countless others. Alain Locke, a

Harvard-educated writer, critic, and teacher who became known as the "dean" of the Harlem Renaissance, described it as a "spiritual coming of age" in which African Americans transformed "social disillusionment to race pride."[20] Langston Hughes called it an "expression of our individual dark-skinned selves."[21] There were also cultural revolutions in other northern cities like Los Angeles, Cleveland, and Chicago, producing such talents as Gwendolyn Brooks, Arna Bontemps, and Lorraine Hansberry.

Unfortunately, while these movements and artists left lasting, powerful, and positive impressions on generations, the heavy financial support and influence of a Black movement by people who were *not* Black resulted in an enormous amount of history and cultural expression excluded from school textbooks or whitewashed altogether. Many of these artists died broke, their work only fully appreciated decades after their deaths.[22]

Nevertheless, Dr. Woodson took on the responsibility of catapulting the emphasis on the study of more Black history into the people's collective consciousness. As one of the first African Americans to receive a doctorate from Harvard, Dr. Woodson dedicated his career to the field of Black history. We bestow to him credit for founding Black History Month. He will forever be respected as having delivered to the nation the incredible work of celebrating, honoring, and promoting Black history and culture when minimal history was being taught.

## CHAPTER FOURTEEN

## What You Didn't Learn about Lewis Howard Latimer

Everyone knows that Thomas Edison created the light bulb. However, he was not the first or only person who tried to invent the incandescent light bulb. Humphry Davy (1802) and Joseph Wilson Swan (1850) are two people who are also said to have contributed to its invention.

Still, it wasn't until Lewis Howard Latimer invented the carbon filament that the world would see something like the longer-lasting light bulb used today.

Lewis Latimer was born in Chelsea, Massachusetts, on September 4, 1848. He was the youngest of four children born to parents who had escaped slavery in Virginia six years before Latimer's birth. His father, George Latimer, who was captured and defended by abolitionists Frederick Douglass and William Lloyd Garrison, purchased his freedom. Sadly, George disappeared shortly after the Dred Scott decision in 1857.[1]

Due to his father leaving, Latimer stepped up to support his mother and siblings. In 1864, at sixteen, he lied about his age to enlist in the US Navy during the Civil War. Latimer was honorably discharged and began working at the Crosby and Gould patent law office, where he taught himself mechanical drawing and drafting. His talent soon captured the attention of Thomas Edison and Alexander Graham Bell. Latimer worked with these men on the groundbreaking invention of the light bulb and helped Graham draft the patent for his telephone design. He also designed his own creations, including an improved railroad car bathroom and an early air conditioning unit.[2]

On October 14, 1878, Thomas Edison filed his first patent for "Improvement in Electric Lights." The problem with these lights was that they had a short life span and were too hot, making them inefficient in houses and businesses. Edison continued to test several types of material for metal filaments to improve his original design.[3]

Latimer developed a carbon filament for the fluorescent lightbulb while working at the US Electric Lighting Company alongside renowned inventor Hiram Maxim. Electric illumination became more feasible and economical for the typical household thanks to the development. Following this discovery, Thomas Edison's company, Edison Electric Light Company, started selling light bulbs that were made for commercial use in 1880.⁴

# CHAPTER FIFTEEN

## What You Didn't Learn about the Harriet Tubman (Mis)Quote

Harriet Tubman's exact birth date is unknown, but estimates place it between 1820 and 1822 in Dorchester County, Maryland. She was born Araminta "Minty" Ross to Harriet Green and Benjamin Ross, later adopting her mother's name after escaping slavery. Tubman's enslavers rented her out to neighbors as a domestic servant at five.[1]

Early signs of her strength came when she intervened to keep her master from beating a man who tried to escape. She was hit in the head with a two-pound weight, leaving her with a lifetime of severe headaches and narcolepsy. Tubman experienced spells, dream-states, and visions she would later contribute to helping her to flee.

She was deeply spiritual but also endured seizures, and severe headaches for the remainder of her life.[2]

In 1978, Cicely Tyson played Harriet Tubman in *A Woman Called Moses*.[3] Released in 2017, the film portrayed two naive scientists who discovered a way to bring people back from the past featuring a Tubman character. The most recent movie, *Harriet*, was released in 2019 and starred Cynthia Erivo.[4]

Tubman's life and words have transformed the world. Celebrities, leaders, and everyday people have used one powerful quote. I have used it, and you have probably used it, too: "I freed a thousand slaves. I could have freed a thousand more if only they knew they were slaves."[5]

However, as powerful and noble as these words are, there is no evidence Harriet Tubman said them. Additionally, while we can be sure the records of the time did not count the exact number of people Tubman freed, in her own words and extensive documentation on her rescue missions, we know that she freed about seventy people during approximately thirteen trips to Maryland.[6] During public and private meetings in 1858 and 1859, Tubman repeatedly told people she freed between fifty and sixty people before her final mission in 1860, when she freed another seven.[7]

One of the earliest attributions of the quote to Tubman is from Sarah Bradford, who exaggerated the numbers in her 1868 biography.[8] Although Tubman is said to have worked with her,

Bradford never claimed that Tubman gave her those numbers; rather, Bradford guessed it.[9]

Robin Morgan, a white feminist who penned the 1970 essay, "Goodbye to All That" is also known for attributing the quote to Tubman.[10] She updated this essay in 2008 during the US Democratic Party's primary presidential candidate race between Hillary Clinton and Barack Obama. The phrase returned to public consciousness when Morgan used a variation of the quote to challenge women who did not support Clinton, saying, "Let a statement by the magnificent Harriet Tubman stand as a reply. When asked how she managed to save hundreds of enslaved African Americans via the Underground Railroad during the Civil War, she replied bitterly, 'I could have saved thousands—if only I'd been able to convince them they were slaves.'"[11]

The implication was that women who did not support Hillary Clinton were similarly enslaved and did not know it.

Milton Sernett, professor emeritus of history and African American studies at Maxwell School, African American studies at Syracuse University, and author of *Harriet Tubman: Myth, Memory, and History*, shared this comment with history blogger, Ralph Luker, who first queried the quote: "My impression is that this is a late 20th-century quote from a fictionalized account of Tubman's life. Whoever wishes to use the dubious quote as a political zinger ought to cite a reliable source."[12]

Kate Clifford Larson, author of *Bound for the Promised Land: Harriet Tubman, Portrait of an American Hero*, said that the quotation was recent, and no evidence backed that Tubman spoke these words. According to Larson, the phrase was entirely made up, did not have an original quote, and only started to gain popularity in the 1990s. He claims that neither historical nor documentary support exists for this quotation.[13]

There is a cultural image of Tubman running around, a gun over her shoulder, and people behind her as she leads them to the promised land. However, she didn't do this as often as Americans would like to believe. It was too dangerous for her to travel all over the South to free the enslaved alone. She returned to Maryland to rescue her family. Then, she used The Underground Railroad—a network of African American and white people offering shelter and aid to escaped enslaved people. She advised slaves to flee on Saturdays because owners took Sundays off and would not discover missing slaves until Monday, giving the slave a two-day advantage. She also liked to relocate when the days were shorter in the winter.[14]

**If Harriet did not *say* she *freed a thousand slaves*, what *did* she say?**

These words were documented at an 1896 suffrage convention in New York City: "I was the conductor of the Underground Railroad for eight years, and I can say what most conductors can't say—I never ran my train off the track, and I never lost a passenger."[15]

Harriet Tubman's knowledge of towns and transportation routes made her attractive to Union military commanders during the Civil War, and she became a Union spy and scout. She wore disguises like that of an older woman to walk the streets under Confederate control and to learn about Confederate troop placements and supplies from the Black people who were still enslaved. She helped many of these people find food and shelter. Tubman was also a nurse administering herbal remedies to Black and white soldiers dying from infection and disease.[16] (If she did say she freed thousands, this could be what she meant.)

Tubman's heroism was so extraordinary that she later became known as "the Moses of her people" for her commitment to leading them to freedom.[17] Just as the Hebrew Moses led the children of Israel out of Egypt and into the Promised Land, Tubman led Black people out of slavery in America.

"General Tubman," as she was also called,[18] lived to be ninety-one, and her birthname revealed her life's purpose. Araminta is a cross between Aminta and Arabella, meaning prayer and protection, and in Hebrew, it means lofty. Not only did Tubman free her people from slavery, but she raised money to help freedmen and cared for her aging parents.[19] She worked with writer Sarah Bradford on her autobiography as a source of income, married a Union soldier, cared for the elderly in her home, and adopted a daughter in 1874.[20]

Tubman was so powerful that she refused anesthesia when she had brain surgery, opting instead to chew on a bullet, just like Civil War soldiers did when they had a limb amputated.[21]

Harriet Tubman died in 1913 and was buried at Fort Hill Cemetery in Auburn, New York, with full military honors.[22]

# CHAPTER SIXTEEN

## What You Didn't Learn about Anna Murray Douglass

Frederick Douglass has become a household name in Black history; however, before Douglass was renowned, his wife Anna Douglass helped this powerful man become the man we know today. Helen Pitts, Frederick Douglass' second wife, formed the Frederick Douglass Monument and Historical Association, which depicted Frederick as a singular great man within an integrated antislavery and Black civil rights movement.[1] However, the Douglass children emphasized the centrality of their Black family in supporting his work. They cast the domestic work of their mother as part of their father's political activism.[2] As Frederick's wife for forty-four years, navigating raising five children with a largely absent husband and tasked with much of the unseen labor of fighting racism, Anna deserves her credit.

Frederick and Anna met in 1838 when he still went by the surname Bailey, and she went by Murray. Anna was the first of her siblings to be born free after her parents were freed. At seventeen years old, Anna left home for Baltimore, where she worked with a French family for two years. Upon leaving this household, Anna served another family and, over the years, gained the reputation of a thorough and competent housekeeper. Over the years, Anna managed to earn and save money, and when she met Frederick, she was financially prepared to start a life with him.[3]

But first, he needed freedom.

To help him escape, Anna used her savings and sold a bed to pay for Frederick's train tickets. He had tried to escape before, but it was not until Anna helped him that he was successful. Anna's expertise in helping her husband escape could have had something to do with her work helping to care for families who had escaped to the Underground Railroad years prior. On May 29, 1832, she and several of her family members, possibly siblings, applied for Certificates of Freedom that would allow them to travel out of Maryland unmolested.[4] In a speech given in 1900, that later became the book *My Mother As I Recall Her*, Anna and Frederick's daughter Rosetta Douglass Sprague stated that Anna brought almost everything the couple needed to start their life together, including a feather bed with pillows and linens, dishes with cutlery, and a full trunk of clothes for herself.[5]

By borrowing a freedman's protection certificate from a friend and wearing the disguise of a sailor that Anna had sewn, Frederick made his way to New York City by train. Once there, he sent for Anna, and they were married in the home of abolitionist David Ruggles.

Anna was largely illiterate and left behind little evidence of her life. Thus, Rosetta's account remains one of the few pieces written about her mother. On the contrary, Frederick wrote thousands of letters, spoke to hundreds of crowds, and wrote several books. Why didn't he teach Anna to read when he did it so well? We would never know for sure. Anna most likely preferred privacy over the national popularity of her husband. This woman grew up when the Black body was never safe or private—a place where the body could be beaten, raped, surveyed, violated, and sold. There is also the politics of homelife for Anna, given her husband's career. She was raising a family while her husband rose to prominence in the anti-slavery struggle and eventually in national politics, which brought a variety of visitors to their home for varying amounts of time.[6] Anna and her children enjoyed the same economic stability Frederick enjoyed, and Anna still made her own money. The Douglass's enjoyed cultural norms denied to most Blacks at that time.[7] We also know that as Frederick became more and more involved in the abolitionist movement, he became more absent. He travelled extensively to give speeches, including two years in England from 1845 to 1847, with Anna left alone to raise and support the family. During this time,

Anna saved everything Frederick sent back and used her own money from mending shoes to support the family. Sprague recalled that "Father was mother's honored guest."[8]

As Frederick became more involved in activism, his relationship with Anna became more strained. She could barely read and write and felt out of place among Frederick's friends, most of whom were highly educated and openly looked down on Anna.[9] She enjoyed being part of the Black community in New Bedford, but in 1847 Frederick moved the family, and as his circle of friends widened, hers diminished. Additionally, on two occasions, Frederick had women he was rumored to be sleeping with move into Anna's house, causing controversy between the couple and within Frederick's political community.[10] The most famous incident is the accusation of William Lloyd Garrison, who charged Frederick with engaging in an interracial, extramarital affair with his business manager, Julia Griffiths, who had been a guest in the Douglass home.[11] This accusation pulled Anna into the public eye. She gave a carefully worded denial, and Harriet Beecher Stowe and Janet Swisshelm came to her defense.[12]

How Anna felt about the perceived scandal is something no one can say. We only know the two ended in divorce, after which Frederick married Helen, a white woman. Whatever for sure went on in that household, and the extent of Anna's role as abolitionist and helping with the movement behind the scenes is something Anna Douglass took to her grave.

Anna Murray Douglass died of a stroke in 1882 at the family home in Washington D. C. She was first buried at Graceland Cemetery in Washington, D. C.; however, the cemetery closed in 1894, and she was moved to Mount Hope Cemetery in Rochester, New York. Frederick Douglass was buried next to her after his death on February 20, 1895.

# CHAPTER SEVENTEEN

## What You Didn't Learn about the Unsung Women of the Harlem Renaissance

There are some names that we are familiar with when it comes to The Harlem Renaissance. Black American history would never be the same without outstanding writers like Langston Hughes and Zora Neale Hurston. However, there are many more names we should know but that we are not taught in school. Many of them had works published in the *Opportunity*, an academic publication run by the National Urban League that is credited with promoting the Harlem Renaissance literary movement.[1]

## Clarissa Scott Delany

Born in 1901 in Tuskegee, Alabama, Delany is most known for her powerful poem "The Mask."[2] After her young years in Alabama, Clarissa was sent to New England, where she graduated from Wellesley College in 1923. During Delany's years at Wellesley, she attended Boston Literary Guild meetings. Each week, speakers were featured, and Delany began writing and gained their attention. This led to her eventual association as a writer of the Harlem Renaissance movement.

Dying at the early age of twenty-six, she contributed to the Harlem Renaissance by also publishing poetry and journal articles in *Opportunity*.

## May Miller

May Miller (also known by her married name of Sullivan) was the most widely read playwright of the Harlem Renaissance. May was raised in an intellectual family; her father was the first Black student to enroll at Johns Hopkins University. She frequently related tales of giving up her childhood bedroom so W. E. B. Du Bois, the author of The Souls of Black Folk, and the poet Paul Laurence Dunbar could visit. She discussed the trips made by Booker T. Washington, Carter G. Woodson, and Alain Locke.[3]

As an intellectual, Miller graduated from Howard University in 1920, earning an award for her one-act play *Within the Shadows*. Nevertheless, her play, *The Bog Guide (1925)*, helped to catapult her into the Black cultural scene as the most published woman playwright of the Harlem Renaissance. Part of her appeal to Black audiences was how she openly addressed racial issues in her plays.

In *Scratches* (1929), she commented on color and class bias within the Black community. *Stragglers in the Dust* (1930) focused on African Americans in the military, and *Nails and Thorns* (1933) dramatized lynching. She also wrote many historical plays (including *Harriet Tubman* and *Sojourner Truth*) that were anthologized in *Negro History in Thirteen Plays* (1935).

## Marita Bonner

One of four children, Marita Bonner, was born in Boston to Joseph Andrew and Mary Anne Bonner. She was raised and educated in Boston, attending Brookline School, where she received musical training. In 1918, she entered Radcliffe College, concentrating on English and comparative literature.[4]

In Washington, Bonner became closely associated with poet, playwright, and composer Georgia Douglass Johnson. Booner also began to publish her writing in journals like *The Crisis* of the NAACP and *Opportunity*. Her first published pieces, "Hands" and "On Being Young-a Woman-and Colored," appeared in *The Crisis* in 1925.

## Dorothy West

Dorothy West was the daughter of a freed enslaved couple named Isaac and Rachel West. West's father built a fruit and vegetable business that gave the family a more affluent life among Boston's middle class. Langston Hughes nicknamed West "The Kid." She also shared an apartment with Zora Neale Hurston and was a young member of the Harlem Renaissance. She was almost twenty, when she won a prize from the *Opportunity* for her short story "The Typewriter" in 1926; West moved to Harlem and joined poets, novelists, musicians, and other artists.[5]

West's work was set apart in that it explored the aspirations and conflicts of middle-class Blacks. West was one of the last surviving members of the prominent group of Black artists, writers, and musicians who flourished in New York City's Harlem district during the Harlem Renaissance before her death in August 1998.

# CHAPTER EIGHTEEN

## What You Didn't Learn about the Chicago Black Renaissance

The Harlem Renaissance, the literary, musical, and artistic movement that exploded during the 1920s in Harlem, New York, is a well-known cultural phenomenon. Also known as The New Negro Renaissance, the New Negro Movement, the Negro Renaissance, and the Jazz Age, the Great Migration of Blacks from the South to northern cities like New York produced a national movement centered on Black culture and tradition. As discussed in chapter thirteen, the movement brought music, literature, art, and theatre to the mainstream from a Black perspective in a huge way. Magazines employed Harlem Renaissance writers on their editorial staff, published their poetry and short stories, and promoted African

American literature through article reviews and annual literary prizes.

Though termed *Harlem* Renaissance, the movement was much more widespread than Harlem itself. While standing as the anchor for the movement, Harlem was just one piece of a much larger puzzle. Across the United States and the Caribbean, *the renaissance* was taking place. Many artists were native to Harlem, but a Black Metropolis brewed in other major cities, such as Chicago.

As the Harlem Renaissance wound down, the Chicago Black Renaissance began, or rather, continued. Creativity and activism bloomed from the significant number of Blacks moving from the South to escape Jim Crow and the Great Depression. Those who had come to Chicago from southern states, like Mississippi and secured well-paying jobs, found they were no longer available. While at first, Blacks could work at factories, meat packing places, and steel mills, the Great Depression ended these opportunities.

African Americans also dealt with deplorable living conditions and fought housing discrimination. As more Black people moved to Chicago, the city also increased its European immigrant population. This made competition for jobs fierce, and because of segregation, many Blacks found themselves unemployed. However, great beauty often springs from the depths of struggle, and the Black Mecca of Chicago's South Side was quite literally a diamond in the rough.[1]

The Black Belt of Chicago's South Side, as it was called, was the location for such diamonds. Jazz, blues, and literature flourished as an outlet for African Americans to voice their discontent about the city and their experiences in the United States. Written in 1959 and published in her 1960 book *The Bean Eaters*, Gwendolyn Brooks wrote the poem "We Real Cool," after walking by a pool hall full of boys in her Chicago neighborhood. Instead of asking herself why they weren't in school, she imagined how the boys felt about themselves.[2] The "we" marking the end of each line in the twenty-four-word poem is meant to be recited softly and swiftly as if the boys shooting pool at the Golden Shovel are questioning their place in the world.[3]

Though never officially deemed the "Chicago Renaissance," Chicago exploded in culture from the 1930s through the 1950s, and the South Side remains the most cultured part of the city today. In 1936, Richard Wright (born in Mississippi but moved to Chicago in 1927), founded the South Side Writers Group[4] to provide a space for encouragement and inspiration for budding writers.[5] In 1940, his classic novel *Native Son* was born, catapulting him into national prominence.

Other artists included the following: Frank Yerby, Margaret Walker, Willard Motley, John H. Johnson (publisher of *Ebony*), St. Clair Drake, and Horace R. Cayton (who later co-authored *Black Metropolis*), and Lorraine Hansberry. Well-known entertainers were Nat King Cole, Ray Nance, and Oscar Brown Jr. Dancers included Katherine Dunham and Talley Beatty. Photographer

Gordon Parks and the artists Elizabeth Catlett and Hughie Lee Smith were also a part of the Chicago Renaissance.

# CHAPTER NINETEEN

## What You Didn't Learn about Ida B. Wells-Barnett

Ida B. Wells was born into slavery on July 16, 1862, in Holly Springs, Mississippi.[1] Although born enslaved, Wells was born to politically active parents during Reconstruction. Her father, James, was involved with the Freedman's Aid Society and helped found Rust College.[2] The purpose of the Freedmen's Aid Society was to increase education opportunities for freed Blacks in the South, including men, women, and children.[3] The society established schools and colleges for southern Blacks, increasing literacy rates by the end of the nineteenth century. Rust, a historically Black liberal arts college, is one of those schools.

It is clear from an early age that Ida B. Wells was destined to become politically active like her parents when she was expelled from Rust College for a dispute with the university's president.[4]

She lost both her parents and younger brother to an outbreak of yellow fever that had decimated Holly Springs.[5] No longer enrolled as a student, Wells convinced the school that she was eighteen and began teaching to support her siblings.[6]

Ida B. Wells and her siblings moved to Memphis, Tennessee, where she lived with an aunt and continued to teach. She also attended classes at Fisk University in Nashville.[7] She would take a train during her commute from Memphis to Nashville, and in May of 1884, a train crew tried to convince her to move to the Black-only part of the train, although she had bought a first-class ticket.[8] Like Rosa Parks and her predecessors, Ida refused, and they forcibly removed her from the train. Wells sued the railroad and won a $500 settlement in a circuit court, although the Tennessee Supreme Court later overturned the decision.[9]

Later, Ida's friends (Tom Moss, Calvin McDowell, and Will Stewart) started a grocery store that drew customers away from a white-owned store in the neighborhood. The white storeowner and his supporters clashed with Moss, McDowell, and Stewart on multiple occasions. One night, they guarded their store against an attack and shot several white men.[10] The three were arrested and taken to jail. Unfortunately, they did not have a chance to defend themselves. A lynch mob took them from their cells and murdered them.[11] Wells wrote articles decrying the murders and risked her own life traveling to the South to gather information on other lynchings.

Inspired by these events, Wells turned her attention to writing about race and politics. Her work was published in several Black-owned newspapers and periodicals under the pseudonym "Lola." She also held shares of *The Free Speech* and *Headlight and Free Speech* newspapers.[12] Wells was vocal about the segregation of the Memphis School District in which she worked and was fired from her teaching job in 1891 for her criticisms.

After the murder of her friend and his two business associates, Wells reported heavily on the epidemic of lynching in the South. Exposing these lynchings resulted in an attack on her press; white mobs burned it down, while she visited Philadelphia. Wells then left Memphis for Chicago.[13]

Chicago residents are familiar with the Ida B. Wells Projects in the heart of the Bronzeville neighborhood on the south side of Chicago, which tells us that Wells-Barnett did not stop her political fight when she moved up North. In 1893, she joined other Black leaders in calling for the boycott of the World's Columbian Exposition, accused of locking out African Americans and negatively portraying the Black community.[14]

In 1895, Wells married Ferdinand Barnett, a famous lawyer with whom she had four children, and continued her fight for freedom. Despite being a wife and mother, Wells-Barnett formed several civil rights organizations, including the National Association of Colored

Women. She was an advocate for women's suffrage, particularly for Black women, and founded the Alpha Suffrage Club in Chicago on January 30, 1913. In 1909, Wells-Barnett attended a conference for an organization that would later become the National Association for the Advancement of Colored People (NAACP). However, Wells-Barnet cut ties with the organization because it lacked action-based initiatives.[15]

Ida B. Wells died of kidney disease on March 25, 1931, in Chicago and left behind a powerful legacy of social and political activism.

## CHAPTER TWENTY

## What You Didn't Learn about Mary Beatrice Davidson Kenner

Mary Beatrice Davidson Kenner was born in Monroe, North Carolina, on May 17, 1912, and came from a family of inventors. With a sister who invented a children's board game and a father who patented a pants presser, it was apparent from the beginning that inventing was in Kenner's blood. When the family moved to Washington, DC, Mary continued to draw and check the US Patent and Trademark Office to see whether someone had already patented her inventions.[1]

Kenner enrolled at Howard University but dropped out due to financial constraints. To make ends meet, she held various jobs and became a federal employee during World War II. After the war, Kenner became a professional florist while inventing in her free time.

In 1951, she married James "Jabbo" Kenner, and the couple fostered five children.

Kenner went on to patent numerous inventions that made life easier, including the toilet paper roll and the sanitary belt. The belt, created in 1957, was her first invention and used to hold sanitary napkins in place. Previously, some of the most common forms of protection for women were grass, rabbit skins, sponges, rags, menstrual aprons, homemade knitted pads, and other homemade absorbents.[2] Usually, women used some form of cloth, giving birth to the phrase "she's on the rag," a popular (and for some women derogatory) expression used to refer to women who are menstruating. At the time, the menstrual period was still considered taboo and many women made their own forms of protection at home.

Despite creating a revolutionary solution for women, a company that showed interest in Kenner's invention rejected it after discovering she was a Black woman. Kenner's material hopes and dreams were dashed due to the company's racism.[3] Consequently, the sanitary belt didn't become widespread until thirty years after its design.

Kenner received five patents for her invention between 1956 and 1987. Maxi pads (a sticky side that stuck to the lining of a woman's panties) were invented in the 1970s, so the sanitary belt lasted only a short time.[4] But without the belt, someone would not have thought to make things easier by replacing the belt with the napkin. And while tampons existed, using them for younger women was considered sexually improper at the time.[5]

While she is known for the sanitary belt, Kenner had other groundbreaking creations, such as a serving tray and soft pocket attached to a walker, a back washer attached to a shower wall, and the toilet paper roll.

Mary Kenner died in 2006 in Washington DC. She was ninety-three years old.

# CHAPTER TWENTY-ONE

## What You Didn't Learn about Phillip L. Downing

The mailbox is a critical part of our lives today. However, if you time-traveled and met anyone before the 1800s, they wouldn't know what a mailbox was. In the early 1800s, people went to the post office to retrieve mail. During chattel slavery, this is how news quickly spread. The person the enslaver sent to the post office to get the mail would linger long enough to get a drift of the conversation from the group of white people who congregated there. On his way back to the big house, the mail carrier would retell the news he heard so that the enslaved knew what was happening in the world. Then, Black people would pass the information along, popularizing the phrase, "I heard it through the grapevine."[1]

While records accredit the expression to the news that came through the telegraph, the "grapevine telegraph" was unofficially invented first as mouth-to-mouth rumors, gossip, and worldly conversations and news of the war from southern Blacks on the plantation.[2]

When mail began to be delivered to homes, the mailbox became necessary due to the overwhelming amount of mail people received. In 1858, Albert Potts patented a letter box where people could leave their mail.[3] However, his small box required people to empty it frequently. Anyone interested in mailing a letter still had to make long trips to the post office.

That is until 1891.

Phillip Downing was born in Providence, Rhode Island, on March 22, 1857. His father, George T. Downing, was an abolitionist and business owner. His grandfather, Thomas Downing, was born to emancipated parents in Virginia and had a successful business in Manhattan's financial district in 1825. Thomas Downing also helped found the United Anti-Slavery Societies of New York City.[4]

Coming from a family of business owners, it's no surprise that Downing would become an inventor. During the late nineteenth and early twentieth century, Downing successfully filed five patents with the US Patent Office. Among his most significant inventions were a street letterbox and a mechanical device for operating street railway switches, which he invented before the predecessor of today's mailbox.[5]

On June 17, 1890, the US Patent Office approved Downing's application for "new and useful Improvements in Street-Railway Switches."[6] His invention allowed the switches to be opened or closed using a brass arm next to the brake handle on the car's platform.

Philip Downing designed a much bigger metal box with four legs which he patented on October 27, 1891.[7] He called his device a street letter box, the predecessor of today's mailbox.

Downing's design resembled old-school mailboxes with a tall metal box with a secure, hinged door to drop letters. His invention allowed for drop-off near one's home and easy pick-up by a letter carrier, instead of someone traveling to the post office. His idea for the hinged opening prevented rain or snow from entering the box and damaging the mail.[8]

Philip Downing died in Boston on June 8, 1934. He was seventy-seven, with several patents under his belt, including a device that utilized a roller and a small, attached water tank to dampen envelopes he patented on January 26, 1917.

# CHAPTER TWENTY-TWO

## What You Didn't Learn about the Brown Paper Bag Test

Throughout US history, variations in skin tone have reflected social status and hierarchies. During slavery, mixed-raced children born of white and Black ancestry experienced privileges not afforded to non-mixed-raced children. Sometimes the enslaver would feel sorry for the kids he knew were his and free them because they were family.[1] As a result, having a fair complexion was valued in the society of the enslaved.[2]

After slavery, family ties to the enslaver provided these children with advantages over their non-mixed brothers and sisters in obtaining education, higher-paying jobs, and property. Consequently, to maintain access to such privileges, many prominent biracial men and women continued to marry those mixed as they were or white.

Passing, when a person classified as a member of a racial group (in this case, African American/Black) is accepted or perceived ("passes") as a member of another (in this case, European/white), was common for most fair-skinned Blacks.[3]

Over the years, passing has been accurately portrayed in the media. For example, in *Beyond the Colored Line*, Book 2 in my Black historical fiction series, I explore the depths of racial passing where Stella changes her name to Sidney McNair, marries a white man, and has biracial children she raises as white. This narrative is taken directly from historical accounts of lighter-skinned Blacks passing and living as white. Other media that explored this topic includes Nella Larsen's novel *Passing* turned Netflix film, Tyler Perry's *A Jazzman's Blues*, and Charles W. Chesnutt's *The House Behind the Cedars*.

Colorism is prejudice or discrimination against individuals with a dark skin tone, typically among people of the same ethnic or racial group, where lighter skin is treated more favorably than darker skin. Colorism not only affected Black people's social lives, but also their occupations. Nadra Kareen Nittle wrote that "In black America, those with light skin received employment opportunities off-limits to darker-skinned blacks. This is why upper-class families in black society were largely light-skinned."[4]

Jack and Jill of America was founded in 1938 with the goal of empowering young people through civic engagement, charitable giving, leadership development, and volunteer work.[5] In the beginning, Jack and Jill, like many African American sororities and fraternities, had a reputation as a prominent group for those who were once regarded as, almost literally, the cream of Black society, according to a *Pittsburgh Courier* article.[6] It made it easier for Black kids from homes with lighter skin to blend in with white America.

Data from the National Survey of Black Americans (1979-80) revealed that complexion was a significant predictor of occupation and income.[7] Results indicate that darker-skinned Black people had continuing disadvantages due to persistent skin discrimination among the Black bourgeoise or Black elite.[8] Over time, people immediately noticed a Black person's skin tone and recognized it as a critical component in joining churches, fraternities, sororities, and other social interactions.[9]

Harvard historian, Henry Louis Gates Jr. outlined the practice of skin discrimination in his book *The Future of the Race*. In his experience, he recalled that "Some of the brothers who came from New Orleans held a bag party. As a classmate explained it to me, a bag party was a New Orleans custom wherein a brown paper bag was stuck on the door. Anyone darker than the bag was denied entrance."[10]

The paper bag test was used to determine who was acceptable based on colorism or color bias. Social experiments were created for entry that favored Eurocentric features such as the comb test, (measuring if the hair was straight enough to go through a comb) and the Brown Paper Bag Test.

The Brown Paper Bag Test, known widely as "The Paper Bag Test," was a form of racial discrimination practiced within the African American community in the twentieth century by comparing an individual's skin tone to a brown paper bag. If a person's skin tone matched or was lighter than the brown bag, they would be more likely to be accepted than a person whose skin tone was darker than the paper bag.

Many famous Black clubs and social organizations, including employers, used this test to determine membership. Brent Staples, an American writer, observed colorism during his research of the 1940s. Staples noticed that Black job candidates frequently described themselves as having light skin. Sometimes 'light colored' was mentioned as the major requirement instead of experience, references, and other crucial information for cooks, drivers, and waitresses. They did it to increase their chances and reassure white employers who might find consumers with dark complexion undesirable.[11]

Later, Spike Lee created his film *School Daze* to demonstrate how colorism had grown in the Black community. Black sorority women disagree over which group has the nicest skin and hair color. The Gamma Rays in the movie have to be "paper bag light."[12]

In the television series *Mixed-Ish*, the spin-off of *Black-ish* starring Traci Ellis Ross, In the 1980s, Rainbow Johnson describes what it was like to grow up in a mixed-race home. She talks about the ongoing struggles she and her family members experienced with choosing between assimilation and remaining true to who they were.

In Season 2, Episode 1, Johan (played by Ethan Williams) allowed his peers to think he was Mexican, thus passing for Mexican. Alicia's (Tika Sumpter) sister Denise (Christina Anthony) remarks that Rainbow's parents had indirectly caused this by living in a community where race, specifically Blackness, was not discussed or considered. "You all taught that poor boy of being ashamed of being Black," says Denise, "You took him to that commune where...nobody talked about race, and that taught him not to be proud of his Blackness."[13]

Origins of colorism, which produced such practices as the paper bag test, can be traced back to another source on the banks of the James River in Jamestown, Virginia, in 1712.

*The Willie Lynch Letter* is a document that a British slaveowner wrote to US enslavers that explained how to control their slave population. In it, the following is advised: "You must use the dark skin slaves vs. the light skin slaves, and the light skin slaves vs. the dark skin slaves."[14] While there is an ongoing controversy about the legitimacy of *The Willie Lynch Letter*, the effect that the concept of race and colorism has had on the African American community cannot be denied. Whether Willie Lynch wrote these words or not, here is what has occurred:

- Early European scientists used eugenics to "prove" race was real by adapting classifications for humans typically reserved for animals.[15]

- White US settlers created a hierarchy that favored Eurocentric features over the darker races.

- A racial hierarchy has been used against African Americans to such an extent that it created divisions within the Black community based on whose skin color was closer to white, which was deemed the more superior race.

- This racial hierarchy is referred to in our present terminology as colorism.

The paper bag test was a manifestation of colorism, which was used to segregate lighter-skinned slaves from darker-skinned slaves during slavery. Passing this test meant being accepted and having access to social and educational opportunities.

The practice of passing happened where Black people who were fair skinned passed or masqueraded as whites.

# CHAPTER TWENTY-THREE

## What You Didn't Learn about the Fultz Sisters

Mary Louise, Mary Ann, Mary Alice, and Mary Catherine were medical miracles. Born on May 23, 1946, at Annie Penn Hospital in North Carolina, "The Fultz Quadruplets," were the first globally recorded identical Black quadruplets and the first set of quads to survive in the South. Born into a tenant farming family in North Carolina, the girls were named by their white doctor, who called them after his family members: his wife Marry-Ann, aunt Mary Alice, daughter Mary Louise, and great aunt Mary Catherine.

If that weren't odd enough, Dr. Klenner negotiated a deal with PET Milk company (now PET Milk, Inc.) that provided all medical expenses, food, land, a house, and a live-in nurse to care for the girls. At the time, Black people were excited about the opportunity:

> [Mr. Fultz] had never made more than $500 a year in his whole life. So, when Pet came around with that offer, Mr. Fultz and the others thought they'd had a blessing from heaven. You've got to remember that all that was more than 20 years ago in the rural South, and anything that white people did for you in those days was kind of unusual. And to think that after all those years, the Fultz family would have a 150-acre farm and their own house just given to them by a big company way off in St. Louis. Why, everyone down there thought that was just marvelous. (Sanders, 1968)[1]

Klenner created a schedule where people could visit the quads through a glass screen.[2] He also tested his theories of vitamin C on the girls the day they were born, injecting them with 50 milligrams each.[3] Next, Klenner sold the rights to use the sisters for marketing purposes to the highest-bidding formula company.

The Fultzs had six other children without a car, electricity, phone, or running water. James Fultz was a sharecropper, and Annie Mae Fultz lost her ability to hear and speak in childhood.[4] Mr. and Mrs. Fulz were poor, and the girls were born in a segregated wing of the hospital, which was the basement. The family lived in poverty, while PET Milk's profits from a previously untapped market of Black families skyrocketed.

Charles and Elma Saylor adopted the quads and moved them to Yanceyville. Their travels became more frequent as they became "national icons of the post-war baby craze and of the birth of the black urban consumer,"[5] appearing in countless PET Milk advertisements into their teenage years. They flew to Chicago at the invitation of Ebony publisher Johnnie Johnson, who featured them on his cover four times. They also appeared in Chicago's star-studded Bud Billiken Parade, went on TV with Roy Rogers and Texas Pete, and would go on to appear in many more ads and make TV appearances. At thirteen, the quads performed as a string quartet in the annual Orange Blossom Festival in Miami, Florida, and at sixteen they were featured in a PET Milk ad for an autographed picture. Many remember them most from their visit to meet former Presidents Harry S. Truman and John F. Kennedy.

As they grew from infants to young ladies, the quads were still employed as PET Milk spokespersons. The first company to sell nonfat dry milk was PET Milk, which was an improvement on the 1920s-era powdered milk.[6] The milk's highest sales year ever was 1950, due to the promotional campaign for The Fultz Sisters, which became a national sensation due to their rarity.[7] Even their siblings, who stayed on the farm while the girls traveled and made appearances on TV and in publications, thought the sisters were wealthy.[8]

"They always thought they were better than us," said their older sister Doretha.[9] However, the public perception of their success was not the truth. According to a 1099 statement submitted by First

National Bank, in contrast to the white Dionne Quintuplets, who earned $1 million in a trust fund at age seven,[10] the quads' Pet profits in their 18th year came to $11.97, which was to be shared four ways.[11]

According to Charles L. Sanders of *Ebony* magazine, the highly publicized PET Milk advertising contracts only brought in $350 a month. Saylor, the girls' foster mom, testified to how much they struggled. "Out of that $350 came my salary," Saylor said, and adding that the acreage given to the girls was so poor, it was hard to grow anything on it. "Somebody ought to just take a trip down to North Carolina and inspect that great farm that was played up so much in the newspaper stories," she told Ebony. "It's in the middle of nowhere, and the land's so poor that you can't even get timber to grow on it anymore. Then the place has always been so hilly that you couldn't raise good crops on it." They also gave the girls a house, but it was not all it was cracked up to be in the media. "Let's set the record straight," continued Saylor. "It was an old four-room place in which 13 to 14 people, including myself as the babies' nurse, had to live. Pet [sic] Milk put in a faucet and electricity and a gas hot plate for cooking, and they closed in the front porch so that I'd have a place to sleep. That was, I guess you'd call it, the 'nurse's quarters'—my room, out there on the porch."[12]

Black people did not have ownership of their children during slavery, just as they did not have ownership of themselves. Because they were his property, the enslaver gave them his surname. Similarly, Dr. Klenner altered the names of the girls to reflect his own family, as if he owned them. Then, like slaves on an auction block, he sold the rights to use the sisters for marketing purposes to the highest bidding formula company. Klenner displayed the Quads behind glass, much like Londoners did with Sara "Hottentot Venus" in the 1800s and Samuel Verner did with Ota Benga at the Bronx Zoo in 1906.

It was now the 1940s, and nothing had changed.

Dr. Klenner and the US government took advantage of the Fultz family in the same way an enslaver ruled over those he enslaved.

Legal, political, and social barriers have regularly prevented Black mothers from choosing how to feed their children since slavery. In *Skimmed*, Andrea Freeman reveals how feeding America's youngest population is rife with social, legal, and cultural injustices, while narrating the captivating tale of the Fultz quadruplets.[13]

The story of the quads is also the story of the government's propaganda of manipulating women to trust formula over breastfeeding. As the money from PET Milk rolled in, so did people's trust in formula and distrust of breastfeeding.[14]

Ironically, after a lifetime of marketing formula instead of breast milk, each Fultz sister developed and died from breast cancer later in life.

# CHAPTER TWENTY-FOUR

## What You Didn't Learn about Rosa Parks' Predecessors

Born Rosa Louise McCauley on February 4, 1913, in Tuskegee, Alabama, Rosa Parks was forty-two years old on December 1, 1955, when she refused to give up her seat for a white passenger.[1]

Parks' name and legacy are cemented in history as the woman who became the catalyst for the Montgomery Bus Boycott. Just four months after the brutal lynching of Emmett Louis Till shocked the country, Parks' arrest officially began what would become known as the civil rights movement. However, there is much about her role our history books left out. Rosa Parks was a seasoned freedom fighter who grew up in a family that supported Marcus Garvey. Her grandparents were strong advocates for racial equality as formerly enslaved people, and in 1932 at nineteen years old, Rosa McCauley married Raymond Parks, a barber, and supporter of the Scottsboro boys.[2] Raymond Parks was also already an active member of the National Association for the Advancement of Colored People (NAACP) when the two met. Through Raymond Parks, Rosa would also start working with the NAACP as the Montgomery chapter secretary and youth leader.

The media has given us the perception that Parks was elderly and quiet. The truth is she was only forty-two years old in 1955, had been a voice for the inhumane treatment of African Americans, referred to Malcolm X as her hero, and according to her autobiography, was not tired with hurting feet from working at the department store when she refused to give up her seat.[3]

The NAACP had been searching for a woman to represent the movement for years, and civil rights activists planned and orchestrated the act of Parks not giving up her seat to end bus discrimination.[4] Before Parks, several other Black women who challenged bus segregation filed lawsuits, and some of them were considered but the NAACP did not choose them.

### Irene Morgan

Eleven years before Rosa Parks, a Black woman named Irene Morgan, later known as Irene Morgan Kirkaldy, was arrested in Middlesex County, Virginia, in 1944 for refusing to give up her seat on a Greyhound bus to state law on segregation.

It was July 16, 1944, when twenty-seven-year-old Morgan traveled by bus from Virginia to Baltimore when she was arrested for refusing to give up her seat for a white passenger. As segregation laws stipulated, Blacks had to sit in buses' and trains' "colored only" section.[5] Even still, if it got crowded and white passengers could not find seats in the whites only section, they had the authority to sit in the colored section. If Black passengers were already seated, they had to give up their seats to the white passengers.[6]

This happened when Morgan and a woman next to her were asked to give up their seats to a white couple. Morgan refused. "Under Virginia law at that time, racial segregation was mandatory on state-sponsored transportation. Ms. Morgan insisted that her presence on an interstate bus meant that Virginia law did not apply, and she refused to be removed from her seat. Police physically dragged the young Black woman from the bus, held her in the Saluda City Jail, and convicted her of violating the state segregation law."[7]

The Irene Morgan Decision inspired the men and women of the Congress of Racial Equality (CORE) to create a nationwide protest movement called the "Journey of Reconciliation." The movement involved groups of civil rights activists who rode buses and trains across states in the South in 1947, a precursor to the Freedom Rides of 1961.[8]

The *Irene Morgan v. Commonwealth of Virginia* handed down a landmark decision on June 3, 1946, when they agreed that segregation violated the Constitution's protection of interstate commerce. *Irene Morgan v. Commonwealth* mobilized further court rulings and the civil rights movement.[9]

Eight years later, the Supreme Court decided in *Brown v. Board of Education* that segregation violated equal rights protection.

Irene Morgan died on August 10, 2007.

## Claudette Colvin

Born on September 5, 1939, in Montgomery, Alabama, Claudette Colvin refused to give up her seat to a white passenger months before Rosa Parks on March 2, 1955. After refusing to relinquish her seat, Colvin was dragged off the bus screaming, "It's my constitutional right!"[10] Colvin said that she felt like Sojourner Truth was pushing down on one shoulder and Harriet Tubman was pushing down on the other—saying, 'Sit down girl!'"[11]

Colvin was arrested for violating Montgomery's segregation laws and one count of assaulting an officer. The NAACP considered using Claudette, but at just fifteen-years-old, they thought she was too young. The organization also dismissed the idea because she was pregnant, and they did not want to represent a young, unwed mother and bring about negative attention to the movement. "They said they didn't want to use a pregnant teenager because it would be controversial, and the people would talk about the pregnancy more than the boycott," said Colvin.[12]

Claudette Colvin served as a plaintiff in the landmark legal case *Browder v. Gayle*, which helped end the practice of segregation on Montgomery public buses.

Today, Claudette Colvin is not a name we often hear, but she, too, played a role in challenging bus segregation.

"I wanted the young African-American [sic] girls also on the bus to know that they had a right to be there, because they had paid their fare just like the white passengers," she told *Time* magazine.[13] "This is not slavery. We shouldn't be asked to get up for the white people just because they are white. I just wanted them to know the Constitution didn't say that."[14]

## Aurelia Browder

After Colvin, Aurelia Browder followed suit and was arrested on April 19, 1955, for refusing to give up her seat. Browder was born on January 29, 1919. She was a member of the NAACP, the Southern Christian Leadership Conference (SCLC), the Women's Political Council (WPC), and the Montgomery Improvement Association (MIA). While Browder may seem to be a likely candidate given her affiliations with several civil rights organizations, the NAACP didn't think she was ideal to lead the movement with six children and no husband.

As a graduate of Alabama State University, a seamstress, and the lead plaintiff in the *Browder v. Gayle* case challenging the Alabama state statutes and Montgomery city ordinances requiring segregation on Montgomery busses, Browder was another steppingstone toward choosing Rosa Parks.

Fred Gray and Charles D. Langford filed the case on behalf of four Black women, who were mistreated on city buses. The case made its way to the US Supreme court, which upheld a district court ruling that the statute was unconstitutional.[15]

## Mary Louise Smith

Mary Louise Smith was born in 1937 in Montgomery, Alabama, and graduated from St. Jude Educational Institute. On October 21, 1955, at the age of eighteen, Smith returned home on the Montgomery city bus. At a stop after Smith had boarded and was seated, a white passenger boarded. There was no place for the white passenger to sit, and the driver ordered Smith to give up her seat. She refused. Smith was arrested and charged with failure to obey segregation orders and given a nine-dollar fine. Like Colvin, Smith was rejected as someone to lead the movement for bus desegregation because she was too young. There were also rumors that her father, who paid the nine-dollar fine, was an alcoholic.

Smith's story came to light during the *Browder v. Gayle* case, where she was one of the women represented. After her refusal to give up her seat on the bus, Smith, her sister, and their children were part of a class-action lawsuit for desegregation of the Montgomery YMCA. Smith was also part of the March on Washington in 1963, and the Dr. King led march from Selma to Montgomery in 1965.

Morgan, Colvin, Browder, and Smith were followed by Susie McDonald and Jeanetta Reese.

After the events of December 1, 1955, Rosa Parks lost her job and received death threats. The NAACP also awarded her the Presidential Medal of Freedom and the Congressional Gold Medal. Nevertheless, while Parks was the public face of bus desegregation, several other Black women helped pave the way for the eventual groundbreaking bus boycott.

# CHAPTER TWENTY-FIVE

## What You Didn't Learn About Dr. Martin Luther King Jr.

Dr. Martin Luther King Jr. is one of the most quoted and talked about Black leaders of our time, and his "I Have a Dream" speech catapulted him deeper into the national spotlight. As a social activist, Baptist minister, key player in the civil rights movement, and the driving force behind the Montgomery Bus Boycott of 1955 and the 1963 March on Washington, as well as helping to bring about such landmark legislation as the Civil Rights Act and the Voting Rights Act, Dr. King's works as an icon are well known. Before his assassination on April 4, 1968, he was awarded the Nobel Peace Prize (1964) and is remembered annually around his January 15th birthday, a US federal holiday since 1986.

But, how much do we know about Dr. King, the *man*?

## Michael King Jr.

In Atlanta, Georgia, Dr. Martin Luther King Jr., was born Michael King, the second of three children born to Michael King Sr. and Alberta Christine on January 15, 1929.[1] Michael Jr. was born and raised on 501 Auburn Avenue in the Sweet Auburn neighborhood, then home to some of the country's most prominent and prosperous African Americans and now part of the MLK Birth Home Tour of the National Historical Park. King's grandfather Reverend Adam Daniel Williams, Alberta's father, purchased the house in 1909.

Michael King Sr. changed his and his son's name to Martin after one of the sixteenth century Protestant Reformers, Martin Luther. He did this after touring Germany and witnessing the beginnings of Nazi Germany while in Berlin.[2] The Ebenezer Baptist Church sent King Sr. to Europe in 1934 for a Baptist World Alliance meeting. The meeting was in Berlin, but King Sr. also traveled to Rome, Tunisia, Egypt, and Jerusalem.[3] Adolf Hitler had become chancellor the year before King's arrival, according to the Martin Luther King Jr. Research and Education Institute at Stanford.[4]

## Gifted

Dr. King was extraordinarily gifted, skipping the ninth and twelfth grades and going straight to Morehouse College at just fifteen-years-old. In 1948, King graduated from Morehouse at nineteen years old with a degree in sociology and enrolled in Crozer Theological Seminary in Chester, Pennsylvania. While attending Crozer, he also studied at the University of Pennsylvania. King was elected President of the Senior Class, delivered the valedictorian address, and won the Pearl Plafker Award for the most outstanding student. He began doctoral studies in Systematic Theology at Boston University in 1951. While in Boston, he met Coretta Scott, a singer from Alabama who was studying at the New England Conservatory of Music.[5] The couple married in June of 1953.

Dr. King also studied at Harvard University and received his doctoral degree on June 5, 1955. From 1957 to 1967, he was awarded numerous honorary degrees from various colleges and universities in the United States and several foreign countries.

## Better Schools for Children in the Cabrini Green Projects

In 1966, Dr. King moved into an apartment on Chicago's west side as part of the Freedom Movement. He was less interested in civil rights then and more in human rights, including fair housing in Northern cities. Chicago in the 1940s, 1950s, and 1960s was a segregated city plagued with a system of redlining that prevented Blacks from purchasing property in their own communities. Richard Wright once referred to kitchenettes as our prison, our sentence to death without a trial, and the new manifestation of mob violence that relentlessly targets the victim and all of us.[6]

In Chicago, run-down apartments were divided into kitchenettes that split six-family apartments in half, becoming one-room apartments.

Public housing (e.g., the Projects) was supposed to be the answer to the slums but did not fare much better. People eventually abandoned public housing for the suburbs, offended that Blacks were being treated as whites.[7] Newspapers and advertisements featured joyful, positive Blacks and Italians coexisting side by side.[8] However, images of whites and Blacks coexisting infuriated white neighborhood dwellers, and riots broke out as whites pulled Black people from their cars and assaulted them. As the screening process grew more relaxed, middle-class African Americans were forced out of public housing. Eventually, the government put up gates (i.e., Robert Taylor and Cabrini Green), but these made residents feel imprisoned. The once "promised land," the newly established public housing program guaranteed, became just another ghetto.[9]

Black schools also suffered. One elementary school was overcrowded, and Dr. King fought with residents to get a racist teacher fired. "The people from Mississippi ought to come to Chicago to learn how to hate," he said after being stoned by angry white residents in the then all-white Marquette Park on the city's southwest side.[10]

When parents were on their third day of a planned strike, King met with them, saying, "Should you in any way be persecuted or prosecuted for attempting to seek the best education possible for your children, I can assure you that thousands of parents from all over the city will come to your aid, and together we will join you in jail if necessary."[11]

## The Poor People's Campaign

Dr. King established the Poor People's Campaign, a program that aimed to unite a multiracial coalition of workers, religious leaders, and the poor to fight poverty in a way that purposefully prioritized the voices of the underprivileged.[12] Officially commencing in December 1967, Dr. King wanted to bring together poor people from across the country to demand better jobs, homes, education, and lives. The campaign's goal was to dramatize the suffering of America's poor, of all races, and make it very evident that they were fed up with waiting for a better life.[13]

King's goal was to provide access to healthcare for all Americans, not just the privileged, this included Black people, who were living in high poverty.[14] Although the campaign succeeded in qualifying 200 counties for free surplus food distribution and securing promises from several federal agencies to hire poor people to help run programs for the poor,[15] King was assassinated on April 4, 1968, days before the official launch on April 22, 1968.

## Campaigned for Black Sanitation Workers in Memphis

Dr. King helped Black sanitation workers in Memphis, Tennessee, in March and April of 1968. He compared their struggle with the Poor People's Campaign, saying that he was campaigning against dehumanization, discrimination, and poverty pay for capable, hardworking people in the wealthiest nation in the world.[16] The deaths of Echol Cole and Robert Walker brought the issue of sanitation workers into the public eye. These men were crushed to death by a trash compensation mechanism on a garbage truck that malfunctioned on February 1, 1968.[17]

The deaths of these men highlighted the dangerous conditions under which garbage truck drivers worked, and the strike brought it to civil rights leaders like Dr. King, while speaking to the union.[18]

## The Boulé

Dr. Martin Luther King Jr. was a member of the Boulé, popularly known as Sigma Pi Phi Fraternity. Described as a formerly secret Black fraternity that honors the material and professional accomplishment of Black men, the fraternity was the subject of a front-page article in the *LA Times* on July 18, 1990.[19]

Founded on May 15, 1904, the Boulé, which means "Council of Chiefs" or "Advisor to the Kings," is a Greek-letter post-graduate fraternity for Black professional men.[20]

These organizations appear harmless and focus on the social justice aspects of their missions, such as fundraising for societal causes and finding ways to give back through anonymous philanthropic acts. However, some allege the organization's true purpose has a lot more to do with the occult than philanthropy. With the details of their activities remaining hidden, the Boulé claims to model itself after its predecessor Skull and Bones (S & B) at Yale, according to Boulé Founder Henry Minton.[21] S & B, an organization that links former US President George W. Bush and Senator John Kerry, has a reputation for allegedly participating in satanic practices. The S & B building is described by Yale professors as a gloomy, nearly windowless brown limestone mausoleum.[22]

The Boulé were among the most powerful and prestigious of the Black community,[23] and sought to recruit only the most intelligent of the Black race, boasting a roster of some of the most notable Black men in the African American community. The six founders include Henry McKee Minton; Algernon B. Jackson, M. D., the first African American graduate of the Jefferson Medical School; Edwin Clarence Joseph Turpin Howard, M. D., who in 1869 was one of the first two Black graduates of the Harvard Medical School; Richard John Warrick, D. D. S., a graduate of the Philadelphia School of Dental Surgery; Eugene Theodore Hinson, M. D., a graduate of the University of Pennsylvania School of Medicine; and Robert Jones Abele, M. D., the first Black graduate of Philadelphia's then Hahnemann Medical College, which is now Drexel University College of Medicine.

They recruited men who were just as influential as they were; many of them from college campuses, with particular attention paid to students of historically Black colleges and universities (HBCUs). Sigma Pi Phi was the first organization in history for Black Americans with college and professional education, according to its founder, Minton. One of the main driving forces behind their group was the need for associations with people who shared their interests and outlook on life.[24]

One of the most significant recruitments was at the Niagara Movement of 1905. Organized just a year after the Boulé's founding, the Niagara Movement (1905-10) was an organization of Black intellectuals led by W. E. B. Du Bois.[25] They called for African Americans' full political, civil, and social rights. This movement drew membership from teachers, lawyers, physicians, ministers, and businessmen. After induction, these men are referred to as Archons. Some of the most notable Archons (other than Du Bois) included Dr. Carter G. Woodson; Charles R. Drew, a physician who developed blood plasma; James Weldon Johnson, author of *Lift Every Voice and Sing* (the Black National Anthem); L. Douglas Wilder, the first elected Black governor of a US state (Virginia); and Dr. Martin Luther King Jr.

Many claim that Dr. King was assassinated not for his work on behalf of civil rights but rather for his opposition to the Vietnam War[26] and the Boulé's secret practices,[27] which supposedly drew condemnation from congressmen, the media, and his own civil rights colleagues.[28]

What is known for sure is that as Dr. King plunged deeper into the Poor People's Campaign, much of his earlier views on integration and civil rights began to change. According to Harry Belafonte, one of the last to speak to him before his death, Dr. King regretted integrating his people "into a burning house." [29] By this, he meant that integration meant little if poor Black people continued to live in poverty, saying: "What does it profit a man to be able to eat at an integrated lunch counter if he doesn't have enough money to buy a hamburger?"[30]

Dr. Martin Luther King Jr. was in Memphis for the sanitation strike when he was assassinated at the Lorraine Motel on April 4, 1968.

# CHAPTER TWENTY-SIX

## What You Didn't Learn about A. D. King

Alfred Daniel Williams King's death occurred during two powerful events. Perhaps, the enormity of these events drove the world to forget about a man who held just as much power and influence on the civil rights movement as his brother.

On July 20, 1969, the world watched as America walked on the moon. In Black America, we were in the middle of the Harlem Cultural Festival, a series of music concerts held in New York City, in Harlem and Manhattan during the summer of 1969 to celebrate Black music, culture, and pride. Also known as Black Woodstock, it is the subject of the documentary *Summer of Soul* that aired on Hulu. The film is appropriately named as the festival featured a star-studded line-up, including Nina Simone, Stevie Wonder, Sly and the Family Stone, B. B. King, the Staple Singers, the 5th Dimension, and Gladys Knight and the Pips. Some call it "The Revolution that Could Not Be Televised" because the footage was just recently discovered.[1]

Filmmaker Hal Tulchin documented the entire Harlem Cultural Festival in that year, believing that the soundtrack—Nina and Stevie—and the setting—a post-MLK assassination Harlem—would combine to create a feature-length film that would help establish the series of uptown Manhattan concerts as defining moments in history.[2] However, the concert did not continue past 1969. While Woodstock would be ingrained in America's memory, Black Woodstock would fade away in the background like a forgotten historical footnote.

And so did the legacy of Dr. Martin Luther King Jr.'s brother.

Alfred Daniel "A. D." King, the father of Alveda King, was born on July 30, 1930, in Atlanta, Georgia. On June 17, 1950, he married Naomi Barber, with whom he had five children. Like his brother, A. D. graduated from Morehouse College, but Alfred was less interested in academics. Although he eventually yielded to the calling of a pastor, he initially resisted ministry. A. D. was more interested in the streets, and his grassroots connections would come in handy later in life when he would help to recruit people for civil rights demonstrations.

While Dr. King knew the boardroom and could maneuver his way around intellectuals, A. D. was street smart and responsible for organizing many of the marches King is famous for, becoming known as a master strategist.[3] He had a gift for leading the youth and had his ear to the ground about what the people wanted, and MLK depended on him heavily. Alfred faced many of the same struggles as his brother and several other civil rights leaders during the 1950s and 1960s, including being arrested in an October 1960 lunch counter sit-in in Atlanta.[4] A. D. and his wife also escaped a bombing of their home.[5] Bombings happened so often in the Black community during that time that Birmingham had been nicknamed Bombmingham.[6]

Rev. A. D. and Dr. King not only looked alike, but also sounded alike and were nicknamed "Sons of Thunder" by Martin Luther King Sr.[7] A. D.'s personality is also said to have been relaxing with a sense of humor. However, although his activism mirrored MLK's, A. D. did not like the limelight and had no intentions of usurping that authority from his brother. Friends and family say A. D. King was humble and was not worried about walking in his brother's shadow. "Not being in the public eye never seemed to affect him, but because he stayed in the background, many people never knew that he was deeply involved, too," one of his associates was quoted as saying.[8]

Instead, A. D. played his part and let MLK play his. He supported Martin one hundred percent while staying in his lane. Not only did A. D. help to organize many of the marches, but he also founded the Kentucky Christian Leadership Council (KCL) and served as chairman from 1965 until 1968. The Fair Housing Act of 1968, signed into law by President Johnson, was modeled after Kentucky's open housing ordinance pushed by the KCL.[9]

When Dr. Martin Luther King Jr. was murdered on April 4, 1968, it hurt A. D. deeply, and he never recovered, as he felt it was his responsibility to protect his brother, A. D.'s widow, Naomi King, once recalled.[10] He was present in Memphis when his brother was killed and vowed to find out who murdered him. But on July 21, 1969, at the age of thirty-eight, just a year-and-a-half after Martin's death, A. D. mysteriously drowned in the family swimming pool.[11]

There is much mystery surrounding the death of A. D. According to MLK's daughter Bernice, A. D. was "a very good swimmer."[12] Derek King, A. D.'s son recalled emergency workers' responses to his father's death: "Ain't no water in his lungs," one of them said. "He was dead before he hit the water."[13]

As Neil Armstrong walked on the moon and hundreds of Black people gathered at what became known as "Black Woodstock," A. D. King passed away, and his life and legacy remain just as private in death as they did in life.

# CHAPTER TWENTY-SEVEN

## What You Didn't Learn about Robert Taylor

African Americans entered northern cities like Chicago in large numbers. Their population in the city more than doubled between 1910-1920, from 44,000-109,000.[1] It then doubled again in the next decade, reaching half a million by 1950.[2] African Americans thought escaping the Jim Crow South would lead them into the Promised Land of the North, but this couldn't be further from the truth. Black people were still discriminated against, living in the poorest areas of the city known as slums, and in a different real-estate system than their white counterparts.[3]

To keep newly arrived African Americans out of their neighborhoods, white Americans formed restrictive covenants, legally binding contracts that specified that homeowners could not rent or sell the home to Black Americans.⁴ Redlining was part of that system, which prohibited Blacks from purchasing property in their own communities. Therefore, most African Americans in Chicago settled in the "Black Belt" between the Twelfth and Seventy-ninth Streets and Wentworth and Cottage Grove Avenues.⁵ This area was decrepit and nearly uninhabitable. Landlords charged high rents in poor apartment homes and split six-family homes into one-room apartments. In these overcrowded wood-framed dwellings, fires and deaths were rampant. Lorraine Hansberry's *A Raisin in the Sun* depicted these conditions. Hansberry's drama follows an African American family's attempts to leave the ghetto and settle in a better area. The play, which takes place between 1945-1959, depicted many tensions surrounding racial and housing issues in Chicago at the time.⁶

Many interracial riots occurred in Chicago between 1945-1950 over real-estate race wars and fights over housing.⁷ The Projects, or federal housing, were supposed to be the answer to the turbulence.

Robert Rochon Taylor was born in Cleveland, Ohio on April 12, 1899. He was the son of the first African American to graduate from the Massachusetts Institute of Technology (MIT) and the grandfather to Valerie Jarrett, who was the senior advisor to former US President Barack Obama. He studied architecture at Washington, D.C.'s Howard University (1916-1919). After graduating with a Bachelor of Science in business administration in 1925, Taylor moved to Chicago, focusing less on architecture and more on the real-estate insurance business.⁸

By the early 1930s, Taylor worked with local Black businessmen to form the Illinois Federal Savings & Loan Association, one of only two savings and loan institutions that provided mortgages to Black owners on the south side of Chicago.[9] Thirteen south side Black leaders pooled their resources of $7,000 in 1934 to found Illinois Federal Savings & Loan. Their goal was to aid people in purchasing properties in areas of the city where white-owned banks would not provide financing. Robert Taylor, a property manager who subsequently rose to the position of chairman of the Chicago Housing Authority, was one of the group's members.[10]

Robert Taylor became an activist and Chicago Housing Authority (CHA) board member in 1935 and chairman in 1939. The Robert Taylor Homes were named after him. However, the homes differed significantly from Taylor's vision for the city. He believed in safe and affordable housing for Black Chicagoans and sought to build homes in nicer neighborhoods. Unfortunately, these neighborhoods were in all-white communities at the time, and Taylor's vision was rejected.[11] The 1949 Federal Housing Act, signed into law by the Truman Administration, provided financing for the construction of additional public housing units, with a good number going to Democratic Chicago. Taylor quickly came up with a list of the locations he planned to construct. The majority of them were in white communities on unoccupied land. White Chicago's neighborhood improvement groups reacted angrily to Robert Taylor's list.[12]

In 1950, the City Council produced its own list after rejecting Taylor's, which put almost all of the new public housing on top of the State Street slums. Humiliated, Taylor resigned, and ten years later, The Robert Taylor Homes were built on the former site of one of the poorest neighborhoods in Black Chicago. It was just the kind of location Taylor did not want for the new housing. The memorial to Robert Taylor captures the values he fought against for years and found repugnant.[13]

The construction of the Dan Ryan Expressway in 1962 kept the Taylor homes on one side of the fourteen-lane expressway and all-white neighborhoods on the other. Built in rows over ninety-five acres of slum land, Robert Taylor became the largest public housing project in the United States at the time.[14] The homes extended the State Street Corridor of Public Housing from the Hilliard Homes, just south of the Loop, through the Harold Ickes Homes, Dearborn Homes, and Stateway Gardens. When it opened, Taylor housed up to a peak of 27,000 people, although they were built to maintain only 11,000 people. They comprised twenty-eight high-rise buildings, sixteen stories each, and 4,415 units, mostly arranged in U-shaped clusters of three, stretching for two miles. Red and white buildings occupied the Bronzeville neighborhood on State Street between Pershing Road (Thirty-ninth Street) and Fifty-fourth Street alongside the Dan-Ryan expressway.

In the beginning, Black people were excited to move into the apartments. They provided much more comfort than kitchenettes and gave the people hope that they could live better lives. For years those red and white buildings and the Sears (now Willis) Tower welcomed people into the city. One former resident said this: "I lived there in the 60s, I remember my neighbors like family. Very fond memories of my childhood growing up in 5352 South State Street...Developed our first crushes, received the first free lunch without telling our parents, in a sense, double dipping as kids, hell the penny candy store like Mr. Johnson or Mr. Cadillac had the best nut chews and mint juleps you could get two for a penny. Our parents worked, all the parents worked unless someone's mom was a housewife."[15]

By 1987, the Robert Taylor Homes had changed. My mother was approved for her apartment at 4947 South Federal, Apartment 802 that year. The buildings were already chronically neglected and underfunded by then (starting in the 1970s). By the time I came of age in the early 1990s, the elevators never worked, incinerators were backed up, and the facilities were infested with rats, roaches, and addicts. We had to double bag everything because our apartment was infested with mice and roaches. By the mid-1990s, Henry Cisneros, secretary of Housing and Urban Development for the Clinton administration, called Bronzeville's Robert Taylor Homes "without question, the worst public housing in America today."[16] Despite the buildings being demolished, their legacy continues to be a painful chapter in Chicago's public housing history.

This was not Taylor's vision.

In a 1966 lawsuit, Dorothy Gautraux, a resident of public housing, claimed that the CHA and the US Department of Housing and Urban Development (HUD) had broken racial desegregation regulations by "concentrating more than 10,000 public housing units in isolated African American areas."[17] The US Supreme Court ruled in Gautraux's favor in 1976, ordering CHA to fix the issue. More than 25,000 people who lived in public housing were incorporated into various Chicago neighborhoods and surrounding suburbs from 1976-1998 thanks to the CHA's Gautraux Assisted Housing Program.

Fortunately for him, Robert Taylor did not live to see his name attached to the perpetuation of poverty those neighborhoods created. He passed away at fifty-seven years old, two years before their construction (1959) and five years before their completion in 1962.

# CHAPTER TWENTY-EIGHT

## What You Didn't Learn about the Black Panther Party for Self-Defense

African Americans entered northern cities excited about the possibility of escaping Jim Crow. During the Great Migration, almost six million Black people moved from the South to northern, midwestern, and western states. Between 1910 and 1940, Black southerners moved to New York, Chicago, and Detroit. However, many African Americans found the North was not the land of milk and honey they thought it was. Racial violence, such as the Red Summer of 1919,[1] arose from white people who were angry about the changes in their communities as millions of Black people poured in from the South to other parts of the country. Hostile race relations emerged, and many Black people lived in poverty. By 1968, two-thirds of the Black population lived in ghettos or impoverished communities, also known as slums.[2]

These economic struggles and brutality of northern cities led two young Black men from Oakland, California, to establish what would one day become the most hated Black revolutionary organization of its time. However, there are misconceptions about who they were and what they stood for.

In *Whitewashing the Black Panthers,* Michael Moynihan argues that PBS's documentary *The Black Panthers: Vanguard for The Revolution* tries to excuse a "murderous and totalitarian cult," saying, "almost anything that reflects poorly on the Panthers is ignored or dismissed, and no critics of the party are included. The story is told entirely through the testimony of former Panthers and sympathetic historians."[3]

However, the Panthers were neither a hate group nor a cult. Despite being portrayed as a militant, Black supremacist hate group, the Black Panther Party (BPP) wrote a ten-point program outlining the details of their belief system that detailed who they were and what they strove to accomplish.[4] The central purpose of creating the BPP for Self-Defense was the power to determine the destiny of their own community.[5] This included sponsoring schools, legal aid offices, sickle-cell testing centers, free breakfast programs for children and the elderly, community protection against police brutality, and more.

## Community Protection

Founded in 1966 by Huey Percy Newton and Bobby Seale in Oakland, California, the Panthers took notice of the police brutality in their lives and the lives of the Black community. They saw police beating Black men, with no consequences. They saw malnourished children who did not have food at home and families who were denied access to proper medical care and education.

Seale and Newton met at Merritt Junior College and were active in political movements there. Following the passion of men like Malcolm X and Stokely Carmichael (who were against the passive resistance movements of men like Dr. King), the young men set out to be examples of what they saw was necessary, whether it was helping the elderly across the street, being human traffic signals, or standing between police and civilians to ensure the laws of California were being adhered to. The Panthers were aware of the laws governing their communities. They ensured civilians and the police understood those laws and acted accordingly.[6]

## Free Breakfast Program

Free breakfast is now part of the government's most extensive welfare program and is a natural expectancy for schoolchildren today, but it was not always this way. Complimentary breakfast in schools was not made permanent until 1975. Part of that revolution was due to the free breakfast program set in place by the Black Panther Party.

The US federal government began to consider serving free school lunches through a two-year pilot program conceived by Kentucky Congressman Carl Perkins. According to the Center for Nutrition Policy and Promotion, Perkins was worried about children in rural areas who awoke early to work in the fields and would come to school hungry.[7] However, the problem with the government's program is that it left out Black children. "They basically said that there was this war on poverty that was supposed to be feeding people, taking care of people, but it wasn't [in the black community]," said Joshua Bloom, a history professor at UCLA and co-author of *Black Against Empire: The History and Politics of the Black Panther Party*.[8] The Panthers realized that Black low-income schoolchildren could not focus on their work on an empty stomach. Thus, while the government was testing out their program, the Black Panthers organized a program of their own that would be specific to the needs of Black children.

The program was successful in increasing students' academic successes, with school officials reporting huge improvements with children who were served free breakfast before school. Ruth Beckford, who helped with the program, later said, "the school principal came down and told us how different the children were. They weren't falling asleep in class; they weren't crying with stomach cramps."[9] The Black Panthers fed an estimated 20,000 children nationally in 1969.[10] With the program expanding to BPP chapters in thirty-six cities, it is widely believed that the federal government increased their efforts after witnessing the success of the Panthers. "I really do believe that the government [expanded] their program because of the work we were doing," said former Black Panther member Norma Amour Mtume.[11] Mtume, now sixty-six, joined the BPP at age eighteen, following an incident in which her first husband, also a Party member, was badly beaten by police in a raid of the BPP's offices in December 1969.

## Medical Care

While the BPP is most notable for community protection, reciting the law, and its breakfast program, it also provided medical care to the Black community by operating medical clinics. The 1965 Medicare and Medicaid Act made it illegal to fund any hospital or medical center that discriminated against minorities.[12] However, hospitals and medical practices did not enforce this law, forcing many Blacks to receive mediocre medical treatment from poorly funded hospitals and clinics. Noticing this, the Black Panthers created the People's Free Medical Clinics (PFMC) in 1968. An alternative to President Lyndon Johnson's Great Society community health centers, the PFMCs opened in Kansas City, Chicago, and Seattle, with ten more clinics opening in 1970.[13] Each regional chapter was responsible for securing financial support for its clinic from nearby businesses, congregations, and medical specialists. They staffed the free clinics with dependable volunteers, including doctors, nurses, pharmacists, lab technicians, and medical students.[14]

PFMC provided services for first aid, childhood vaccinations, and screening for high blood pressure, lead poisoning, tuberculosis, and diabetes. The PFMC's most groundbreaking work came in 1971 when they started screening and educating the community about sickle cell anemia, a genetic disease that primarily affects African Americans. It was revolutionary because the Panther's widespread education about the disease came at a time when the government provided little information, and it caused the US Congress to pass the National Sickle Cell Anemia Control Act of 1972.[15] The Act created national genetic counseling, testing, and research to diagnose and treat sickle cell anemia.

The BPP for Self-Defense contributed so powerfully to the Black community that the FBI established special counter-intelligence programs to neutralize the organization within just one year of formation. Between 1956 and 1971, the FBI employed the COINTELPRO program to look into radical national political organizations in an effort to gather information that would reveal the involvement of foreign enemies.[16] Many of the misconceptions about who the BPP were has originated from the FBI.

It was evident that the US government viewed the Black Panthers as an adversary of the US from the informants who infiltrated the Panthers, to the bombing of their offices, to the killing of their members. According to former FBI director J. Edgar Hoover, this was a Black extremist organization and a menace to the internal security of the United States.[17] Robert James "Little Bobby" Hutton, the first member of the BPP, was gunned down at just seventeen years old. Mark Clark and Fredrick Allen Hampton Sr., aka Chairman Fred Hampton (Chairman Fred), President of the Illinois Chapter, soon followed. The men were murdered in Hampton's Chicago apartment on the west side in an FBI orchestrated armed raid with the Chicago police and state attorney. Hampton, drugged by barbiturates, slept alongside his pregnant wife when the men were killed on December 4, 1969.[18] These are just a few of the many ways the US government attacked the Panthers, who did nothing but work to create change and opportunities for Black people. When we look beyond the military-style berets, guns, and raised-fist salute, we see that the Black Panthers preached Black empowerment, armed resistance to racist violence (including at the hands of police), fed Black children, and provided medical care and protection to the Black community.

# CHAPTER TWENTY-NINE

## What You Didn't Learn about the Events of September 15, 1963

The congregation of the Sixteenth Street Baptist Church in Birmingham, Alabama, was knocked to the ground on September 15, 1963, just before eleven o'clock, when a bomb detonated beneath the church's stairs.[1] It was Youth Day, so five girls—two sisters—were joyfully getting ready for the day's service in the basement.[2] Later, their four bodies were discovered in the wreckage of the bombed-out church, shocking the nation with its magnitude. However, it was not a new endeavor for Klansmen, who were constantly bombing churches and homes in Birmingham, the most segregated city in the United States at the time.[3] White people began the bombings as a campaign to stop Black people from moving into all-white neighborhoods.[4] Governor George Wallace and Birmingham's Commissioner of Public Safety Eugene "Bull"

Conner went the extra mile in their fight to keep the South segregated. Fifty dynamite explosions occurred in Birmingham between 1947 and 1965.[5]

On December 25, 1956, the KKK bombed the home of civil rights activist Rev. Fred Shuttlesworth. Seven years earlier, on May 11, 1963, the home of the Rev. A. D. King was bombed. Two bombs exploded minutes apart. King, his wife, and two children escaped injury, but the front of the brick house was demolished. After leading April and May protests against department store segregation in Birmingham, King was a target. However, this was not just happening to Black civil rights leaders but everyday Black Americans. Middle-class African Americans who had purchased homes in areas deemed "white-only" constantly feared for their lives as bombs and riots erupted during the summer.[3]

Helen Shores Lee, a daughter of NAACP lawyer Arthur Shores, remembered those times on Dynamite Hill. She recalled that their home was attacked twice and that her mother discovered a third case of dynamite in her garden just before it exploded.[4]

The starting point of many marches, the Sixteenth Street Baptist Church was a target because it was where civil rights activists held many meetings during the 1960s. It was also due to the success of the Birmingham campaign of May 10, 1963, that led to the city agreeing to desegregate lunch counters, restrooms, drinking fountains, and fitting rooms, to hire African Americans in stores as salesmen and clerks, and to release the jailed demonstrators. White segregationists opposed this, and violence continued to plague the city, culminating in the blast of the morning of September 15, 1963. The bombing killed four of the five little girls in the basement who were getting ready for service.[5] Four young girls, Denise McNair (eleven), Addie Mae Collins (fourteen), Carole Robertson (fourteen), and Cynthia Wesley (fourteen), had been killed in the explosion when parents hurried to the Sunday school classroom to check on the children. Over twenty other people suffered injuries.[6]

With over 8,000 attendees and Dr. King giving the eulogy, Carole Robertson's family opted out of the joint funeral and held a separate, private funeral for her. Sarah Collins Rudolph, Addie Mae's sister, was also present in the basement with the girls during the explosion. She survived but lost her right eye.

Sadly, Sarah was not the only young person forgotten that day.

On the same day as the church bombing, two little Black boys, Virgil Ware, thirteen, and Johnny Robinson, sixteen, were killed. Virgil was riding on the handlebars of his brother's bike when two white boys, Larry Sims and Michael Farley, were coming from a segregationist (Klan) rally when they decided to scare the Ware brothers. Holding Michael's gun, Larry fired two shots, hitting Virgil in the chest and cheek, and killing him. He died in his brother's arms.[7]

Larry and Michael were charged with second-degree manslaughter and given seven months in jail, and then the judge reduced the sentence to two years of probation. The media focused on Dr. King and the four little girls as Virgil's memory faded into obscurity. Similarly, Johnny Robinson, sixteen, died the same day after participating in a demonstration in the aftermath of the bombing. According to reports, a group of Black kids allegedly threw rocks at a car, where white teens drove by and hurled racial slurs.[8] As Robinson ran, he was shot in the back by a police officer named Jack Parker.

Two grand juries refused to bring Parker to trial, and no one was prosecuted for Robinson's death. His story went largely unnoticed for years until the FBI opened a group of cold cases in 2009.[9]

Six Black children died that day, September 15, 1963—four little girls and two little boys.

# CHAPTER THIRTY

## What You Didn't Learn about Louis Till

Louis Till was born an orphan on February 7, 1922, and grew up in New Madrid, Missouri. Like many Black men of the time, he worked for the Argo Corn Company in Summit "Argo," Illinois. The place was actually called Summit, but the biggest corn processing factory in the world—which produced Argo corn Starch, Bosco Malted Milk, Karo Syrup, and Bosco Malted Milk—made Summit a company town with the locals calling it Argo.[1]

At seventeen years old, Louis Till started dating a young lady named Mamie. Born Mamie Elizabeth Carthan in Webb, Mississippi, Carthan's family left the South during the Great Migration and settled in Argo, Illinois. Her father, Nash, found work at Argo and Alma Carthan joined her husband in January 1924, bringing two-year-old Mamie and brother John with her. They settled in a predominantly African American neighborhood in Summit. Although her parents disapproved, Mamie and Louis continued dating and married on October 14, 1940. Their first and only child, Emmett Louis Till, was born one year later, on July 25, 1941.[2]

Sadly, the Till marriage was not a happy one. Mamie would eventually file a restraining order against Louis for abuse. After repeatedly violating the order, the judge forced Louis to choose between prison and the army. He chose the latter and enlisted in 1943, serving overseas in the Transportation Corps of the US Army during World War II.[3]

Later, Louis and another African American private, Fred McMurray, were found guilty by the army court-martial of allegedly raping two Italian women and murdering one during an air raid in 1944. On July 2, 1945, weeks before his son's fourth birthday, the US Army hung both men.[4]

Louis was only twenty-three years old.

His widow, Mamie Till was told her husband's death was due to willful misconduct.[5] She became frustrated with not being given any more information and rarely spoke of Louis since his death. Louis's only personal item was a ring with his initials on it that the army sent to Mamie Till. She thought Louis would have loved Emmett to have it, so she decided to keep it.[6] She had no idea that it would play a crucial role in her son's impending demise.

No other details were revealed about Louis's murder until the murder of his son.

Emmet Till, visiting his cousins, arrived in Money, Mississippi, on August 20, 1955, and stayed with his great-uncle Moses Wright. On August 24th, Till and his cousins went to Bryant's Grocery and Meat Market, a white-owned store in Money, Mississippi—two hours north of Jackson. Accounts of what happened vary, but the cause of Emmett's death was allegedly wolf-whistling at the storeowner's wife, Carolyn Bryant.[7]

On August 28, 1955, between 2:00-3:00 a.m., Roy Bryant, Carolyn's husband, and J. W. Milam, Bryant's brother, forced their way into Wright's home. They kidnapped Emmett at gunpoint and later murdered him, severely beating the boy with a pistol in a storage shed on Milam's farm in Drew, Mississippi.[8] The men then drove Emmett to the edge of the Tallahatchie River, gouged out one of his eyes, shot him, and tied his body to a seventy-five-pound cotton-gin fan with barbed wire. Then, they dumped his corpse into the Tallahatchie River.[9]

Three days later, Emmett's disfigured and swollen body was found by two boys fishing on August 31, 1955. It had been beaten so severely and weighed down by the cotton-gin fan that he had become unrecognizable. The family only recognized him by his father's signet ring, which he wore.[10]

According to the 2005 documentary, *The Untold Story of Emmett Louis Till*, his cousin Ruthie Mae Crawford testified that Emmett asked for ten cents for bubble gum and put the money in Carolyn's hand while paying for it.[11] This was 1955 Mississippi, the Jim Crow South, where white people did not want Black people looking them in the eyes (an existing law of the time referred to as "Reckless Eyeballing"),[12] let alone touch them. Offended at Emmett's audacity, Carolyn quickly pulled her hand back. During the trial, on September 22, 1955, the judge allowed the defense to call Bryant to testify where she exaggerated this account, saying Emmett grabbed her from behind, put his hands around her waist, and pulled her to himself.[13]

After four days of testimony and sixty-seven minutes of deliberation, an all-white, all-male jury (Blacks and women were not allowed to serve as jurors in Mississippi at the time[14]) acquitted Bryant and Milam of all charges.

On September 2, 1955, less than two weeks after Emmett had embarked on his journey south, the same train he had taken going to Mississippi brought his remains back to Chicago. His mother, Mamie Till-Mobley, demanded an open casket showing his dehumanized body and allowed *Jet* magazine to publish the photos so that everyone would know what had been done to her son. The photos went viral, before there was such a thing, shocking the world.[15]

Having been acquitted of murder, Mississippi decided to try Till's murderers with kidnapping charges. During the trial, J. W. Milam and Roy Bryant both admitted to taking Emmett at gunpoint in the middle of the night out of his great uncle's house.

While the state figured out the angle of the case, the press was informed that Till had "committed rape" in Italy and had been executed. They alleged it would be impossible to try J. W. Milam and Roy Bryant with kidnapping. The logic of the time was that because Emmett was accused of assaulting a white woman, it would look bad for the information about his father assaulting a white woman to surface. It would look bad because of the insinuation that Emmett's behavior ran in the family.[16] Thus, on November 9, 1955, a Mississippi grand jury refused to indict Milam and Bryant on kidnapping charges.[17]

Protected against double jeopardy, the two men would later admit to everything in a 1956 interview with *Look* magazine. They admitted that they had tortured and murdered Emmett and sold the story of how they did it for $4000.[18]

In a chilling turn of events, Mamie lost both her husband and her son for practically the same reason: both were accused of assaulting America's sweetheart, the white woman. Had it not been for Emmett wearing his father's ring, the family probably would not have been successful in identifying his body, and the world would never know what became of him.

Until recently, the details of whom the ring belonged and of Louis's life have been excluded from the story. Many documentaries, news reports, articles, and even first-told accounts of Emmett's death mention the ring as the only way to identify him, but they do not mention details about the man to whom it belonged.

# CHAPTER THIRTY-ONE

## What You Didn't Learn about Mostafa Hefny

In what way can a mistaken identity hinder the lives of Black-skinned people in today's world? Introducing the case of Mostafa Hefny.

Since 1997, Hefny has been fighting to reclaim his identity in a lawsuit against the US government, who told him he was not a Black man.

Race has no real meaning and does not represent a person's true place of origin because eugenicists invented it to demonstrate the inferiority of Black people.[1] The US Census Bureau does not define race in terms of biology, anthropology, or genetics; rather, it defines it as a social category.[2] There are five categories recognized by the Census Bureau:

1. White (people with origins in Europe, the Middle East, or North Africa)

2. Black or African American (Africa)

3. American Indian or Alaska Native, Asian,

4. Native Hawaiian

5. Other Pacific Islander

The census also includes a Hispanic ethnic category.

It is an ethnic category rather than a race category because the Latino community includes many races, such as white, Black, Native American, Asian, and mixed. Ethnicity comprises a person's nationality, heritage, ancestry, land, language, and lineage. Race, however, is based solely on a person's skin color or other external physical characteristics.[3] With this system, anyone from Africa can be considered Black even if they are not African American, and anyone from Europe can be considered white even if they are not European.

This is what happened to Hefny.

For thirteen years, a bilingual resource teacher with Wayne County Detroit's Regional Education Service Agency, Dr. Mostafa Hefny, stated he was Black on his employment records. The Director of Human Resources sent him a letter which was copied to the superintendent, threatening his educational career would be ruined if he did not change his racial classification on his employment records from Black to white.

Hefny was shocked when his government-issued identification classified him as "white." One of the administrators even went so far as to say that if he said he was Black again, no one would hire him, and if hired, he would be running from one job to the next for the rest of his life.[4] Even though Wayne County Regional Educational Service Agency (RESA) provides support and consultant services to all of Wayne County, which was 30 percent Black, the superintendent was white, his four associate superintendents were white, and 95 percent of the administrators and consultants were white.[5]

Wayne County RESA did not fire Dr. Hefny. Instead, they denied him promotion twice, persecuted him, harassed him, called him racial slurs, and psychologically tortured him to the point that he left on social security psychiatric disability, which lasted ten years (1989-1998).[6] Dr. Hefny was hospitalized in psychiatric hospitals twice (1992 and 2000), and all the doctors who treated Dr. Hefny stated that his psychiatric injury was work-related in their medical reports. When Hefny recovered and returned to the workforce, Wayne County RESA followed up on their threats, and he was fired five times in one year.[7]

How could a thing like this happen?

According to the Office of Management and Budget Standards for the Classification of Federal Data on Race and Ethnicity, citizens are designated as white if they have "origins in any of the original peoples of Europe, North Africa or the Middle East."[8] According to CBS, Hefny said that he is descended from the Nubians, the ancient group of Egyptians from the northern part of Sudan and southern part of Egypt.[9] According to the US racial classification system, we are not supposed to realize that Egypt is in Africa, just that it is the Middle East. As such, anyone from the Middle East can be considered white, despite their skin tone.

In *The 1619 Project: A New Origin Story*, Dorothy Roberts noted that racial categories were also created to prevent interracial unions according to a Virginia law passed in 1924, entitled "An Act to Preserve Racial Integrity."[10]

In the ancient world, people did not have racial categories. Instead, they were divided according to their land, language, and culture, not by skin tone and color. The ancient Hebrews, Egyptians, Ethiopians, and Libyans did not speak of Africa even though they were indigenous to that continent. Today, people on the continent of Africa may refer to themselves as Ethiopians, Somalians, Nigerians, Egyptians, and Ghanaians just as people from Europe may identify themselves as Irish, Russians, Greeks, or Swedish.

# CHAPTER THIRTY-TWO

## What You Didn't Learn about the Physical Appearance of the Ancient Israelites and Egyptians

For millennia, theologians and academics have disagreed on the ethnic history of the Israelites and Egyptians. Such debates lead to situations like the one with Dr. Hefny in the previous chapter, a Black Egyptian man categorized as white.

On February 8, 2018, the *Today* show unveiled a reconstructed bust of the Egyptian Queen Nefertiti. In addition to her beauty, Nefertiti is also known for her African ancestry, so people were shocked at the shows choice to present a well-known African queen with pale skin and Caucasian features. Social media, specifically, "Black Twitter" commented on the perceived disrespect with some saying that "Nefertiti DID NOT look like Barbra Streisand in Miami."[1]

The most famous representation of Nefertiti is housed in a museum in Germany[2] and shows a much browner version. However, a sculpture isn't necessary to know the queen was Black. All that is required is a study of the physical appearance of the ancient Egyptians.

According to the Bible, Gn: 10 provides a breakdown of Noah's son's descendants and their nations. Of all the biblical chapters quoted by religious faiths, Chapter 10 isn't mentioned much, nor does it spark any significant inspirations like the Book of Proverbs and Psalms, but Chapter 10 is critical when discussing the nations of the Earth before the concept of a race existed. Here, the focus will be on the descendants of Noah's sons Ham and Shem.

In Hebrew, Ham is Cham (pronounced khawm), which means "hot, burnt, and black."[3] The first-born son of Ham, Cush, forms the Kushite nation. They were also called and known as the ancient Ethiopians.[4]

Ethiopia comes from the Greek word, Aithiopia, "burnt or black face."[5] The Greeks applied this name to the people living south of Egypt. The name Egypt comes from the word Aegyptus, though the Egyptians called themselves Khemet/Kemet, interpreted as "people of the black land."[6] (Kem meant "black" in ancient Egyptian from the rich and fertile black soil).[7] Gerald Massey, English writer and author of *Egypt the Light of the World*, wrote, "The dignity is so ancient that the insignia of the Pharaoh evidently belonged to the time when Egyptians wore nothing but the girdle of the Negro."[8] Sir

Richard Francis Burton, nineteenth-century English explorer, writer, and linguist, agreed, responding that he sent home one-hundred mummied skulls to prove the Africanism of the race.[9]

In *The Natural History of Man*, scientist R. T. Prichard said that "In their complex and many of the complexions and in physical peculiarities, the Egyptians were an 'AFRICAN' race."[10]

Additionally, the ancient Greek historian Herodotus, who visited Egypt in the fifth century B. C. E. saw the Egyptians face-to-face and described them as black-skinned with woolly hair.[11]

Anthropologist Count Constatin de Volney (1727-1820) spoke about the Egyptians that produced the Pharaohs.[12] He later asserted that the ancient Egyptians were native-born Africans, confirming Herodotus' discovery. He argued that by interacting with the Romans and Greeks for many centuries, we can understand how their color may have lost some of its initial vibrancy. Additionally, he stated that the Sphinx's face, with its African traits, may attest to the historical evidence of the origins of the people.[13]

Several sources confirm the physical appearance of the Hamites as those of "African" features. Ham also had the most descendants of Noah's sons, populating Africa and other parts of what is now called the Middle East. Ham undoubtedly gave birth to the African nations through both biblical and historical evidence.[14]

The descendants of Noah's son Shem were also Black.

During Moses' birth, the number of children of Israel was increasing,[15] and the Pharaoh implemented a form of birth control to stop the Hebrew women from having so many children.[16] If the women had girls, they should allow the girl babies to live, but they were supposed to kill them if they had boys. When Moses' mother gave birth to him, she hid him for three months and then, when she could hide him no longer, put him into a wicker basket and let it float down the river.[17]

When the daughter of the ruling Pharaoh came to bathe in the river she saw baby Moses, recognized he was one of the Hebrew babies and decided to raise him as her own son. Moses would live as the grandson of the Egyptian pharaoh for a full forty years.[18] If Moses, the descendant of Shem, was a white baby, how was it possible for him to pass as the grandson of the Black pharaoh? As brought forth from Rudolph Windsor, author of the book *From Babylon to Timbuktu: A History of Ancient Black Races Including the Black Hebrews*, only a Black Moses would have been able to be concealed effectively for any length of time among Black Egyptians.[19]

This is not the only biblical example that the ancient Israelites and the Egyptians looked alike.

The first we see to be called a Hebrew in the scriptures,[20] Abraham, was also a Black man and the father of the Israelite and the Arab Nation. While the lineage, according to scripture, would be through Abraham and his wife Sarah's son Isaac,[21] (which would include Isaac's son Jacob [22] and the twelve tribes of Israel[23]), before Sarah gave birth to Isaac, Abraham had a son with Hagar, their Egyptian handmaiden.[24] Her son, Ishmael, also married an Egyptian woman[25] and we have already established that the Egyptians would be considered a Black people today.

When the Hebrew Joseph interpreted the pharaoh's dream, warning of the famine that would soon come,[26] he was released from prison and made viceroy of Egypt. In other words, Joseph ruled as a Vice President over Egypt, and his wisdom, direction, and preparation set Egypt up to survive the seven-year famine. When his brothers, the children of Israel, visited the land for food, they did not recognize Joseph as their brother to the extent that Joseph was so overwhelmed with emotion looking at his younger brother Benjamin that he had to excuse himself.[27]

These nations, Israel and Egypt, lived together, married, and had children together. Israelites were mistaken for Egyptians several times: Moses being raised by the Black pharaoh, Paul being mistaken as a Black Egyptian, and even the Messiah himself hiding among the Black Egyptians.[29] There are also similarities between the Messiah and Moses. During the time of the Messiah's birth, Herod made a similar decree as the pharaoh of Moses time, that is, to put the baby boys to death. An angel appeared to Joseph to escape this cruelty, instructing him to hide the baby in Egypt, and there they lived until Herodes' death.[30] As was the case for Moses, how could a white skinned baby hide among Black Egyptians and not be noticed?

This information is relevant because it is more proof that race alone has no meaning and does not represent a person's true place of origin. The Israelites looked just like the Black Egyptians in physical appearance, although they are two different nations.

While we use terms like Black and white for understanding's sake, it does nothing to help us to understand where these Black and white people originate.

This, too, is Black history we have not been taught in school.

# AFTERWORD

My husband once received an old, rusted iron from my father-in-law, the kind that needs to be heated on the stove. As my father-in-law's family were sharecroppers, he also showed us a scale they used to weigh the cotton they picked. That captivated me in the same way that museums do. There is something magical about holding old, ageless treasures in your hands as a memorial to a special place in time.

When I wrote a novella in 2015 about a biracial descendant of a former slave discovering the truth about her origins and past, I did not want to stop there. For the upcoming book and Black History Month, I decided to present one historical person or event weekly on Fridays in February.

While *Stella: Between Slavery and Freedom* would not be released until February of 2015, I posted the first Black history article on January 17th. It is less extensive than the articles are now renowned for, but it was the beginning of a fantastic new series that I had no idea would still be alive today.

As the month ended, I continued the series, posting one Black historical truth per week.

This is how Black History Fun Fact Friday was born.

Since then, I have written and published over seventy articles covering Black historical facts, from Black inventors and inventions to the Black communities that prospered. For years, the articles were a hit and became a favorite segment of the blog.

This is when I knew I had to do more with the Black history articles I had published to the blog. Something about allowing those articles to only exist on my computer didn't feel right. I needed to document the history and the journey in a deeper way. I needed to turn them into something concrete that I could pass down from generation to generation. I wanted to create something tangible we could hold and remember, like photo albums and paperback books.

In 2021, I set out to revise all the articles and turn them into a history book. To motivate me, I started in November to coincide with National Novel Writing Month. NaNoWriMo is a 501(c)(3) non-profit organization that gives people resources, structure, community, and support to help them finish their books and achieve their creative goals in an organized and timely manner.[1] Although I was not writing a novel, the challenge would give me the push and accountability I needed to finish my first draft.

The easy part was removing the articles from the blog to a word document. However, I learned quickly that writing a blog post is much different from writing a research book! I had no idea what I had gotten myself into. The work I had before me was enormous, but having already committed to the process, I was more than ready for it.

There was also a part of me that needed to write this book.

People know me in my community as a poet and historical fiction novelist. My love and passion for Black history and people are evident to anyone who spends any significant time with me. Because of this, I am the person people think of when they think of Black history. My little cousin contacted me recently asking about our genealogy. He said that when he thought about it, I was someone who would know. This is typically how people engage with me: asking questions about history or inquiring about my opinion on the latest unarmed shooting, political matter involving Black people or what I think of the latest Black biopic.

But the truth is this is not always fun.

Not only does keeping my "ear to the ground" and remaining current on key events in the Black community, both past and present, take a lot of energy, but I also recognize the weight of the duty and am aware of my own limited knowledge. Like the old saying goes: "A wise man is wise enough to know that he actually knows nothing."[2]

Writing this book was a chance for me to sharpen my own sword as well as teach or convey information to others. I knew I couldn't just copy and paste articles. I had to undertake my own deep dive into history, which included conducting new and updated research because many of the articles were outdated.

Every chapter was not only revised from its original, but it also required its own independent study. There were moments when I needed to read entire books to truly absorb the depth of the information, and other times when I needed to perform profound resting, prayer, and meditation.

Eventually, I realized this was more than a book; it was an experience.

This is eight years of writing material and over two years of new research.

You are holding ten years of study in your hands.

I hope that you have not only learned something new you did not know before, but that the information has also empowered you with the confidence to embrace all that Black American history has to offer beyond what we are taught in school in the mainstream media. I hope you will question what you read and hear about and investigate those truths for yourself.

My greatest hope is that after reading this book, you are equipped with enough information to spark the conversation and, if necessary, participate in your own activism for the continual education and restoration of Black historical truth. For some of us, it is writing and documenting history. For others, it might be participating in politics or education.

Whichever your duty, I hope this book is a start. I do not wish for it to be an ending but a beginning. May it bless the hearts and minds of people outside of yourself. Share it with your children, spouse, colleagues, co-workers, students, family, friends, and young people.

May it be a reawakening, a restoration, or even a song. May the stories of our ancestors strengthen and carry us like the Negro spirituals of old that brought our people North to freedom.

May this work act as its own redemption song.

This is my gift to you. It is my historical relic, rusty iron, and cotton scale.

Many blessings and gratitude.

Yecheilyah

# ENDNOTES

# Black History Facts You Didn't Learn in School

## Chapter One

### What You Didn't Learn About Sundown Towns

1- Loewen, James W. 2018. *Sundown Towns*. The New Press.

2- Ibid.

3- Committee, Anna Centennial. 1954. *100 Years of Progress*.

4- "The Terrible Death of William James | OrangeBean Indiana." 2020. OrangeBean Indiana. OrangeBean Indiana. August 17, 2020. http://orangebeanindiana.com/2020/08/17/the-terrible-death-of-william-james/.

5- Ibid., 4.

6- Ibid., 4.

7- Jaffe, Logan. n.d. "What Readers Told Us About Our Story, 'The Legend of A-N-N-A' — ProPublica." ProPublica. Accessed June 14, 2023. http://www.propublica.org/article/reader-responses-the-legend-of-anna-illinois-sundown-towns.

8- Ibid. 1.

9- McGill, Ann. 2020. "The Movie-Going Experience during Segregation Prompted Blacks to Fight for Better Treatment." Https://Www.Live5news.Com. https://www.facebook.com/live5news/. March 6, 2020. https://www.live5news.com/2020/03/06/movie-going-experience-during-segregation-prompted-blacks-fight-better-treatment/.

10- Berry, Mary Frances. 2008. "'Reckless Eyeballing': The Matt Ingram Case and the Denial of African American Sexual Freedom." *The Journal of African American History*, no. 2 (April): 223–34. https://doi.org/10.1086/jaahv93n2p223.

11- "Welcome to ABHM! - America's Black Holocaust Museum." 2023. America's Black Holocaust Museum. https://www.facebook.com/pages/Americas-Black-Holocaust-Museum/264755283560445. June 14, 2023. https://www.abhmuseum.org/.

12- "About – Poor People's Campaign." n.d. Poor People's Campaign. https://www.facebook.com/anewppc. Accessed June 14, 2023. http://www.poorpeoplescampaign.org/about/.

13- Nitkin, Alex. n.d. "50 Years Ago MLK Lived In, Led Fair Housing Fight From Chicago's West Side - North Lawndale - Chicago - DNAinfo." DNAinfo Chicago. DNAinfo Chicago. Accessed June 14, 2023. http://www.dnainfo.com/chicago/20160125/north-lawndale/50-years-ago-mlk-lived-led-fair-housing-fight-from-chicagos-west-side/.

14- Ibid., 12.

15- "Huey v. the Town of Cicero :: 1968 :: Supreme Court of Illinois Decisions :: Illinois Case Law :: Illinois Law :: US Law :: Justia." n.d. Justia Law. Accessed June 14, 2023. https://law.justia.com/cases/illinois/supreme-court/1968/41089-5.html.

16- "Jim Crow Signs as Symbols of Subjugation, Trophies of Triumph | Berkeley News." 2011. Berkeley News. February 15, 2011. https://news.berkeley.edu/2011/02/15/jim-crow-signs/.

17- Ibid., 13.

18- "February 14, 1946." n.d. Black Quotidian: Everyday History in African-American Newspapers. Accessed June 14, 2023. https://blackquotidian.supdigital.org/bq/february-14-1946.

19- *Los Angeles Sentinel* coverage of the Short case, see: "Violence Threat against Short Must Not Go Unchallenged: An Editorial," January 3, 1946

20- "O. H. Short 4th Fontana Victim Dies: Lacked Interest in Recovery," January 24, 1946

21- "NAACP Brand Fontana Fire As Incendiary; Kerosene Theory Flatly Denied by Arson Expert," January 10, 1946

# Chapter Two

# What You Didn't Learn About the Black Communities that Prospered

## Blackdom

1- Binkovitz, Leah. 2013. "Welcome to Blackdom: The Ghost Town That Was New Mexico's First Black Settlement | At the Smithsonian | Smithsonian Magazine." Smithsonian Magazine.

Smithsonian Magazine. February 4, 2013.
https://www.smithsonianmag.com/smithsonian-institution/welcome-to-blackdom-the-ghost-town-that-was-new-mexicos-first-black-settlement-10750177/.

2- Ibid.

3- Ibid.

4- Editor, Adrian Gomez / Journal Arts and Entertainment. 2016. "Film Explores Founding of New Mexico Town of Blackdom - Albuquerque Journal." Albuquerque Journal. https://www.facebook.com/TheAlbuquerqueJournal/. February 19, 2016. https://www.abqjournal.com/726273/africanamerican-roots.html.

5- "Segregation - Postal | National Postal Museum." n.d. National Postal Museum|. Accessed June 15, 2023. https://postalmuseum.si.edu/exhibition/freedom-just-around-the-corner-segregation/segregation-postal.

## Black Wallstreet

1- "Oil and Texas: A Cultural History | TX Almanac." n.d. Home | TX Almanac. Accessed June 15, 2023. https://www.texasalmanac.com/articles/oil-and-texas-a-cultural-history.

2- Summers, Juana. 2021. "Survivors Of 1921 Tulsa Race Massacre Share Eyewitness Accounts." NPR. May 19, 2021. Survivors Of 1921 Tulsa Race Massacre Share Eyewitness Accounts.

3- Montford, Christina. 2014. "6 Interesting Things You Didn't Know About 'Black Wall Street.'" Atlanta Black Star. https://www.facebook.com/ATLBlackStar. December 2, 2014.

http://atlantablackstar.com/2014/12/02/6-interesting-things-you-didnt-know-about-black-wall-street/.

4. "Does a Dollar Spent in the Black Community Really Stay There for Only Six Hours? - Truth Be Told." 2015. Truth Be Told. December 22, 2015. https://truthbetold.news/2015/12/does-a-dollar-spent-in-the-black-community-really-stay-there-for-only-six-hours/.

## The All-Black Community of Boley, Oklahoma

1- "The Indian Removal Act and the Trail of Tears." n.d. Education | National Geographic Society. Accessed June 15, 2023. https://education.nationalgeographic.org/resource/indian-removal-act-and-trail-tears/.

2- "Boley | The Encyclopedia of Oklahoma History and Culture." n.d. Oklahoma Historical Society | OHS. Accessed June 15, 2023. https://www.okhistory.org/publications/enc/entry.php?entry=BO008.

3- Ibid.

4- Ibid.

5- "The Muskogee Cimeter. (Muskogee, Okla.), Vol. 9, No. 32, Ed. 1, Friday, May 22, 1908 - The Gateway to Oklahoma History." n.d. The Gateway to Oklahoma History. Cimeter Publishing Co. Accessed June 15, 2023. http://gateway.okhistory.org/ark:/67531/metadc70104/.

6- Ibid., 1

7- Ibid.

8- Ibid.

### Eatonville

1- The James Madison Institute. 2017. "The History and Legacy of Eatonville, Florida's Pioneering African-American Town - James Madison Institute." James Madison Institute. December 6, 2017. http://www.jamesmadison.org/the-history-and-legacy-of-eatonville-floridas-pioneering-african-american-town/.

2- Frazier, Charles. 2021. "The Town That Freedom Built: The Story of Eatonville, America's First Official Black Town." WFTV.Com. February 23, 2021. https://www.wftv.com/news/town-that-freedom-built-story-eatonville-americas-first-official-black-town/ECOUW2MQYFCAROHCQI55FS4IF4/.

3- Ibid.

### Fort, Mose, Florida

1- Bullock, James. 2008. "Fort Mose, Florida (1738-1820)." BlackPast. January 22, 2008. www.blackpast.org/african-american-history/fort-mose-florida .

2- Ibid.

### Israel Hill

1- Decker, Francis. 2004. "The Town That Freedom Built | Arts and Culture | Style Weekly - Richmond, VA Local News, Arts, and Events." Style Weekly. Style Weekly. November 10, 2004. http://www.styleweekly.com/richmond/the-town-that-freedom-built/Content?oid=1361204.

2- Ely, Melvin Patrick. 2010. *Israel on the Appomattox*. Vintage.

> It has long been known that the black man, woman, and child were actually the offspring of the ancient Israelites. It's probable that these freed black people in Prince Edward County, Virginia, who established a community on a hill they dubbed Israel Hill were aware of this, as they identified as Israelites. 3- "Israel on the Appomattox," by Melvin Patrick Ely

3- Ibid.

### Mound Bayou

1- Mound Bayou's history a 'Magical Kingdom' residents fight to preserve. Mississippi Today. May 10, 2021. https://mississippitoday.org/2018/05/19/mound-bayous-history-a-magical-kingdom-residents-fight-to-preserve/.

2- Ibid., 2.

3- Ibid., 1.

4- Ibid., 1

### Nicodemus Township in Graham County, Kansas

1- "Nicodemus, Graham County Kansapedia - Kansas Historical Society." n.d. Home - Kansas Historical Society. Accessed June 15, 2023. http://www.kshs.org/kansapedia/nicodemus-graham-county/12157.

2- Ibid.

3- Ibid.

4- Ibid.

5- Ibid.

### Rosewood

1- "Rosewood Massacre - Overview, Facts & Legacy." n.d. HISTORY. Accessed June 15, 2023. http://www.history.com/topics/early-20th-century-us/rosewood-massacre.

2- ———. 2013b. "Welcome to Blackdom: The Ghost Town That Was New Mexico's First Black Settlement | At the Smithsonian | Smithsonian Magazine." Smithsonian Magazine. Smithsonian Magazine. February 4, 2013. http://www.smithsonianmag.com/smithsonian-institution/welcome-to-blackdom-the-ghost-town-that-was-new-mexicos-first-black-settlement-10750177/.

3- Blackdom Resident Henderson, Lucy H. The Chicago Defender (Big Weekend Edition) (1905-1966); Chicago, Ill. [Chicago, Ill]. 21 Dec 1912: 3

**Seneca Village**

1- "The Hidden History of Slavery in New York | The Nation." 2005. The Nation. https://www.facebook.com/TheNationMagazine. October 24, 2005. https://www.thenation.com/article/archive/hidden-history-slavery-new-york.

2- "Slavery in New York." n.d. New York Historical Society. Accessed June 15, 2023. http://www.slaveryinnewyork.org/history.htm.

3- Tours, City Running. 2021. "CITY RUNNING TOURS - Sharing The Story of Seneca Village." CITY RUNNING TOURS. CITY RUNNING TOURS. February 7, 2021.

https://www.cityrunningtours.com/blog/2021/2/6/celebrating-black-history-month-the-story-of-seneca-village.

4- Ibid., 1.

## Chapter Three

## What You Didn't Learn About Black Wallstreet

1- "1921 Tulsa Race Massacre - Tulsa Historical Society & Museum." 2018. Tulsa Historical Society & Museum -.
https://www.facebook.com/TulsaHistory. November 1, 2018.
https://www.tulsahistory.org/exhibit/1921-tulsa-race-massacre/.

2- "Tulsa Race Massacre." n.d. Tulsa Historical Society & Museum. Accessed June 15, 2023.
https://www.nytimes.com/interactive/2021/05/24/us/tulsa-race-massacre.html.

3- Fain, Kimberly. 2017. "The Devastation of Black Wall Street - JSTOR Daily." JSTOR Daily.
https://www.facebook.com/JSTOR.org. July 5, 2017.
https://daily.jstor.org/the-devastation-of-black-wall-street/

## Chapter Four

## What You Didn't Learn About Africa Town

1- "Congress Votes to Ban Slave Importation, March 2, 1807 - POLITICO." n.d. POLITICO. Accessed June 15, 2023.
https://www.politico.com/story/2018/03/02/congress-votes-to-ban-slave-importation-march-2-1807-430820.

2- "Africatown Alabama, U.S.A. | National Museum of African American History and Culture." n.d. National Museum of African

American History and Culture. Accessed June 15, 2023. https://nmaahc.si.edu/explore/initiatives/slave-wrecks-project/africatown-alabama-usa.

3- Local Legacies. n.d. "Alabama: AfricaTown, USA (Local Legacies: Celebrating Community Roots - Library of Congress)." American Memory: Remaining Collections. Accessed June 15, 2023. http://memory.loc.gov/diglib/legacies/loc.afc.afc-legacies.200002671/.

4- "National Archives at Atlanta The Clotilda: A Finding Aid." n.d. Clotilda.Pdf. Accessed June 15, 2023. https://www.archives.gov/files/atlanta/finding-aids/clotilda.pdf.

5- Levenson, Michael. 2021. "Last Known Slave Ship Is Remarkably Well Preserved, Researchers Say." The New York Times. December 25, 2021. https://www.nytimes.com/2021/12/25/us/clotilda-slaveship-africa-alabama.html.

6- Ibid. 2

7- Ibid., 2

8- Elliott, Debbie, and Marisa Peñaloza. n.d. "Exploring the Clotilda, the Last Known Slave Ship in the U.S., Brings Hope." NPR. Accessed June 15, 2023. https://www.npr.org/2022/06/15/1105007375/exploring-the-clotilda-the-last-known-slave-ship-in-the-u-s-brings-hope

9- "Slave Shipwrecks, Underwater Archaeology, Coral Restoration." n.d. Diving With a Purpose. Accessed June 15, 2023. https://divingwithapurpose.org/.

10- Lewis, Labbaron. 2023. Interviewed by Yecheilyah Ysrayl. April 14, 2023. Mobile, Alabama.

11- Visit Mobile. 2023. "Opening Date Announced for Long-Awaited Africatown Heritage House." Welcome To Mobile, AL | Restaurants, Attractions, Arts & Culture. Visit Mobile. February 10, 2023. https://www.mobile.org/articles/post/opening-date-announced-for-long-awaited-africatown-heritage-house/.

## Chapter Five

## What You Didn't Learn about Race Riots in the United States

1- "'An Absolute Massacre' - The New Orleans Slaughter of July 30, 1866 (U.S. National Park Service)." n.d. NPS.Gov Homepage (U.S. National Park Service). Accessed June 19, 2023. https://www.nps.gov/articles/000/neworleansmassacre.htm.

2- "'An Absolute Massacre' - The New Orleans Slaughter of July 30, 1866 (U.S. National Park Service)." n.d. NPS.Gov Homepage (U.S. National Park Service). Accessed June 19, 2023. https://www.nps.gov/articles/000/neworleansmassacre.htm.

3- Leon, H. Prather, and Kenneth Davis. 2006. *We Have Taken a City*. DRAM Tree Books.

4- Keyes, Allison. 2017. "The East St. Louis Race Riot Left Dozens Dead, Devastating a Community on the Rise | At the Smithsonian | Smithsonian Magazine." Smithsonian Magazine. Smithsonian Magazine. June 30, 2017. https://www.smithsonianmag.com/smithsonian-institution/east-st-louis-race-riot-left-dozens-dead-devastating-community-on-the-rise-180963885/.

5- "Red Summer | National WWI Museum and Memorial." n.d. National WWI Museum and Memorial. Accessed June 19, 2023. https://www.theworldwar.org/learn/about-wwi/red-summer.

6- Ibid.

7- "NYCdata | Disasters." n.d. Baruch College -. Accessed June 19, 2023. https://www.baruch.cuny.edu/nycdata/disasters/riots-harlem_1943.html.

8- "Race Riot of 1943 | Detroit Historical Society." n.d. Detroit Historical Society | Where the Past Is Present. Accessed June 19, 2023. https://detroithistorical.org/learn/encyclopedia-of-detroit/race-riot-1943.

9- Ibid.

10- Ortiz, Erik. 2021. "Groveland Four, the Black Men Accused in a 1949 Rape, Get Case Dismissed." NBC News. NBC News. November 22, 2021. https://www.nbcnews.com/news/us-news/groveland-four-black-men-accused-1949-rape-get-case-dismissed-rcna6016.

11- Ibid.

12- Ibid., 10.

13- Ibid., 10.

14- "Watts Riots of 1965." n.d. Encyclopædia Britannica. Encyclopædia Britannica. Accessed June 19, 2023. https://www.britannica.com/event/Watts-Riots-of-1965.

15- Ibid.

16- Rojas, Rick. 2017. "Five Days of Unrest That Shaped and Haunted Newark." The New York Times. July 11, 2017. https://www.nytimes.com/2017/07/11/nyregion/newark-riots-50-years.html.

17- Boissoneault, Lorraine. 2018. "Martin Luther King Jr.'s Assassination Sparked Uprisings in Cities Across America |

History| Smithsonian Magazine." Smithsonian Magazine. Smithsonian Magazine. April 4, 2018. https://www.smithsonianmag.com/history/martin-luther-king-jrs-assassination-sparked-uprisings-cities-across-america-180968665/.

18- Ibid.

19- "New York News - New York Daily News." n.d. New York Daily News. New York Daily News. Accessed June 19, 2023. https://www.nydailynews.com/new-york/crown-heights-riot-gallery-1.2759946.

20- Krbechek, Anjuli Sastry, and Karen Grigsby Bates. n.d. "When LA Erupted In Anger: A Look Back At The Rodney King Riots." NPR. Accessed June 19, 2023. https://www.npr.org/2017/04/26/524744989/when-la-erupted-in-anger-a-look-back-at-the-rodney-king-riots.

21- "Michael Brown Is Killed by a Police Officer in Ferguson, Missouri | HISTORY." n.d. HISTORY. Accessed June 19, 2023. https://www.history.com/this-day-in-history/michael-brown-killed-by-police-ferguson-mo.

22- Lopez, German. 2016. "The Baltimore Protests over Freddie Gray's Death, Explained - Vox." Vox. Vox. July 27, 2016. https://www.vox.com/2016/7/27/18089352/freddie-gray-baltimore-riots-police-violence.

23- Ibid.

24- Silverstein, Jason. 2021. "The Global Impact of George Floyd: How Black Lives Matter Protests Shaped Movements around the World - CBS News." CBS News - Breaking News, 24/7 Live Streaming News & Top Stories. CBS News. June 4, 2021.

https://www.cbsnews.com/news/george-floyd-black-lives-matter-impact/.

25- Ibid.

# Chapter Six

## What You Didn't Learn About the Theory of Evolution

1- Darwin, Charles. 2012. *The Origin of Species by Means of Natural Selection or The Preservation of Favored Races in the Struggle for Life*. Hardpress Publishing. "The Origins of Species."

2- Washington, Harriet A. 2008. *Medical Apartheid*. p.190-19. Anchor.

3- Ibid., p 191

4- Ibid., p 191

5- "Maafa 21 - Black Genocide in 21st Century America - Full Documentary." Live Action. February 22, 2018. Video, 6:30:39, https://www.youtube.com/watch?v=I6XfU8KVkzI.

6- Ibid.

7- Ibid. 5

8- Alexander, James-Edward. 1838. An Expedition of Discovery Into the Interior of Africa, Through the Hitherto Undescribed Countries of the Great Namaquas, Boschmans, and Hill Damaras. Etc. (With Plates).

9- "Ota Benga (ca. 1883–1916) - Encyclopedia Virginia." n.d. Encyclopedia Virginia. https://www.facebook.com/encyclopediava. Accessed June 19,

2023. https://encyclopediavirginia.org/entries/benga-ota-ca-1883-1916/.

10- Ibid.

11- Ibid.

12- "Evolution: Library: Huxley: Darwin's Bulldog." n.d. PBS: Public Broadcasting Service. Accessed June 19, 2023. https://www.pbs.org/wgbh/evolution/library/02/2/l_022_09.html .

13- "Thomas Henry Huxley Quote: No Rational Man, Cognizant Of..." n.d. Lib Quotes. Accessed June 19, 2023. https://libquotes.com/thomas-henry-huxley/quote/lbr2y2a.

14- "Johns Hopkins Magazine." n.d. Accessed June 19, 2023. https://pages.jh.edu/jhumag/0609web/sara.html.

15- Ibid.

16- "Serial and Superficial Suction for Steatopygia (Hottentot Bustle) - PubMed." n.d. PubMed. Accessed June 19, 2023. https://pubmed.ncbi.nlm.nih.gov/7976762/.

**Note:** Steatopygia, from the Greek "steato" meaning "fat" and pygia meaning "buttocks," is defined as excessive fat of the buttocks, usually seen in women and sometimes called Hottentot bustle because it was commonly seen in the Hottentot people of southern Africa.

17- Hottentot Apron - Excessive elongation of the labia minora seen in the Hottentot tribe of southern Africa which. Segen's Medical Dictionary. © 2012 Farlex, Inc. All rights reserved.

18- Writer, Contributing. 2022. "How Sarah Baartman's Hips Went from a Symbol of Exploitation to a Source of Empowerment for

Black Women | FIU News - Florida International University." FIU News. Florida International University. September 13, 2022. https://news.fiu.edu/2021/how-sarah-baartmans-hips-went-from-a-symbol-of-exploitation-to-a-source-of-empowerment-for-blackwomen.

19- Massk. 2018. "Massk® International - How Women Have Historically Made Their Butts Look Bigger." Massk. March 2, 2018. http://beautifulbutt.com/women-historically-made-butts-look-bigger/.

20- Rokeshia Renné Ashley, Assistant Professor of Communication, Florida International University. 2022. "How Sarah Baartman's Hips Went from a Symbol of Exploitation to a Source of Empowerment for Black Women." Yahoo | Mail, Weather, Search, Politics, News, Finance, Sports & Videos. Yahoo. October 23, 2022. https://www.yahoo.com/video/sarah-baartmans-hips-went-symbol-122627107.html.

21- Daley, Suzanne. 2002. "Exploited in Life and Death, South African to Go Home." The New York Times. January 30, 2002. https://www.nytimes.com/2002/01/30/world/exploited-in-life-and-death-south-african-to-go-home.html.

22- Ibid., 21.

23- Lengel, Edward G. 2011. *Inventing George Washington*. Harper Collins.

24- "The Lost Museum Archive." n.d. The Lost Museum. Accessed June 19, 2023. https://lostmuseum.cuny.edu/archive/death-of-joice-heth-new-york-sun-february-24.

25- Reiss, Benjamin. 2009. *The Showman and the Slave*. Harvard University Press.

26- Ibid. 25

27- "Joice Heth (c.1756 -1836) · George Washington's Mount Vernon." n.d. George Washington's Mount Vernon. Accessed June 19, 2023. https://www.mountvernon.org/library/digitalhistory/digital-encyclopedia/article/joice-heth-c-1756-1836/.

28- Ibid., 27.

29- Washington, Harriet A. 2008. *Medical Apartheid.* Chapter 8: The Black Stork. p.190-19. Anchor.

30- Ibid., 29.

31- Margaret Sanger's December 19, 1939, letter to Clarence Gamble. Sophia Smith Collection. Smith College. North Hampton Massachusetts. Also described in Linda Gordon's *Women's Body, Women's Right: A Social History of Birth Control in America.* New York. Grossman Publishers. 1976.

32- Ibid., 29, p. 197.

33- Ibid., 29., p.166.

34- Ibid., 33.

35- "The Maggie Awards Recognize Contributions Made by the Media and Arts That Enhance the Public's Understanding of Reproductive Rights and Health Care Issues." n.d. Planned Parenthood | Official Site. Accessed June 19, 2023. https://www.plannedparenthood.org/about-us/newsroom/campaigns/ppfa-margaret-sanger-award-winners.

36- Marshall, Robert Gerard, and Charles A. Donovan. 1991. *Blessed Are the Barren.* San Francisco: Ignatius Press, 1991, 24-25.

37- Green, Tanya L. n.d. "Negro Project." HE NEGRO PROJECT: MARGARET SANGER"S EUGENIC PLAN FOR BLACK AMERICANS. Accessed June 19, 2023. https://www.issues4life.org/pdfs/negroproject.pdf.

38- Indiana Supreme Court Legal History Lecture Series, "Three Generations of Imbeciles are Enough: "Reflections on 100 Years of Eugenics in Indiana, at In.gov Archived 13 August 2009 at the Wayback Machine.

39- Washington, Harriet A. 2008. *Medical Apartheid*. Chapter 8: The Black Stork. p 197. See also Kline, W. (2014, April 29). Feeble-mindedness. Retrieved September 20, 2022, from https://eugenicsarchive.ca/discover/encyclopedia/535eebe87095aa0000000227

40- "The American Idiot Schools: Disability and Segregation in the Nineteenth Century | Consortium for History of Science, Technology and Medicine." n.d. Consortium for History of Science, Technology and Medicine | Promoting Scholarly and Public Understanding of History of Science, Technology and Medicine. Accessed June 19, 2023. https://www.chstm.org/news/american-idiot-schools-disability-and-segregation-nineteenth-century.

41- "Buck v. Bell (1927) | The Embryo Project Encyclopedia." n.d. The Embryo Project Encyclopedia | Recording and Contextualizing the Science of Embryos, Development, and Reproduction. Accessed June 19, 2023. https://embryo.asu.edu/pages/buck-v-bell-1927.

# Chapter Seven

## What You Didn't Learn About Draptomania

1- Willoughby, Christopher D. E. 2018. "Running Away from Drapetomania: Samuel A. Cartwright, Medicine, and Race in the Antebellum South." *Journal of Southern History*, no. 3: 579–614. https://doi.org/10.1353/soh.2018.0164.

2- Cartwright, Samuel Adolphus. 1851. *Report on the Diseases and Physical Peculiarities of the Negro Race*. New Orleans, Louisiana: New Orleans Medical and Surgical Journal, 1851.

3- Ade, Yewande. 2022. "Black People Resisting Slavery Was Presumed To Be A Sign Of Mental Illness | by Yewande Ade | History Street | Medium." Medium. History Street. June 17, 2022. https://medium.com/history-of-yesterday/black-people-resisting-slavery-was-presumed-to-be-a-sign-of-mental-illness-f1c3e25e770c.

4- Ibid., 3.

5- US Legal, Inc. n.d. "Redhibition Law and Legal Definition | USLegal, Inc." Legal Definitions Legal Terms Dictionary | USLegal, Inc. Accessed June 20, 2023. https://definitions.uslegal.com/r/redhibition/.

6- Ibid., 2.

7- Ibid.

8- James Denny Guillory. "The Pro-Slavery Arguments of Dr. Samuel A. Cartwright." *Louisiana History: The Journal of the Louisiana Historical Association* 9, no. 3 (1968): 209–27. http://www.jstor.org/stable/4231017.

9- Ibid.

10- Washington, Harriet A. 2008. *Medical Apartheid.* Chapter 8: The Black Stork. 2006. p. 61.

11- Anglin DM, Malaspina D. Ethnicity effects on clinical diagnoses compared to best-estimate research diagnoses in patients with psychosis: a retrospective medical chart review. J Clin Psychiatry. 2008 Jun;69(6):941-5. doi: 10.4088/jcp.v69n0609. PMID: 18494534; PMCID: PMC5336694.

12- Svalastog AL, Martinelli L. Representing life as opposed to being: the bio-objectification process of the HeLa cells and its relation to personalized medicine. Croat Med J. 2013 Aug;54(4):397-402. doi: 10.3325/cmj.2013.54.397. PMID: 23986283; PMCID: PMC3763245.

13- Ibid., 12.

14- Khan FA. The Immortal Life of Henrietta Lacks. J IMA. 2011 Jul;43(2):93-4. doi: 10.5915/43-2-8609. Epub 2011 Aug 10. PMCID: PMC3516052.

15- Ibid., 14.

16- Ibid.

17- Development of the Polio Vaccine: A Historical Perspective of Tuskegee University's Role in Mass Production and Distribution of HeLa Cells. Retrieved from https://www.ncbi.nlm.nih.gov/pmc/articles/PMC4458465/

18- Ibid.

# Chapter Eight

## What You Didn't Learn About Uncle Tom

1- "Blackface Minstrelsy | American Experience | Official Site | PBS." n.d. PBS: Public Broadcasting Service. Accessed June 20, 2023. https://www.pbs.org/wgbh/americanexperience/features/foster-blackface-minstrelsy/.

2- Engle, G. D. (1978). This grotesque essence: Plays from the American minstrel stage. Baton Rouge: Louisiana State University.

3- "Uncle Tom's Cabin – Harriet Beecher Stowe Center." n.d. Harriet Beecher Stowe Center. https://www.facebook.com/HarrietBeecherStowe/. Accessed June 20, 2023. https://www.harrietbeecherstowecenter.org/harriet-beecher-stowe/uncle-toms-cabin/.

4- Drew, Benjamin. 2022. "British American Institute – The Refugee: Or the Narratives of Fugitive Slaves in Canada." Toronto Metropolitan University Pressbooks – Open Educational Resources Publishing. Ryerson University. February 15, 2022. https://pressbooks.library.torontomu.ca/therefugee/chapter/british-american-institute/.

5- Reynolds, David S. 2011. "Uncle Tom Revisited: Rescuing the Real Character from the Caricature." Black Past. August 9, 2011. https://www.blackpast.org/african-american-history/uncle-tom-revisited-rescuing-real-character-caricature/.

6- "Malcolm Describes the Difference between the 'House Negro' and the 'Field Negro.'" n.d. Columbia CTL | Columbia Center for Teaching and Learning. Accessed June 20, 2023.

http://ccnmtl.columbia.edu/projects/mmt/mxp/speeches/mxa17.html.

7- "The Tom Caricature - Anti-Black Imagery - Jim Crow Museum." n.d. Jim Crow Museum of Racist Imagery. Accessed June 20, 2023. https://jimcrowmuseum.ferris.edu/tom/homepage.htm.

8- Kev, Chitown. n.d. "Racism and Honorifics or Why I Call Denise Oliver-Velez 'Miss Denise.'" Daily Kos. Accessed June 20, 2023. https://www.dailykos.com/stories/1434792/full_content.

9- Ibid.

10- "Ontario Heritage Trust | Dawn Settlement, The." n.d. Ontario Heritage Trust. Accessed June 20, 2023. https://www.heritagetrust.on.ca/en/plaques/the-dawn-settlement.

11- "Fugitive Slave Act | American Battlefield Trust." n.d. American Battlefield Trust. Accessed June 20, 2023. https://www.battlefields.org/learn/primary-sources/fugitive-slave-act.

12- "A New Interpretation for 'Little Black Sambo' : NPR." 2003. NPR. NPR. December 23, 2003. https://www.npr.org/2003/12/23/1567555/a-new-interpretation-for-little-black-sambo.

13- "Lazy Richard." Jefeester. February 15, 2013. Video, 0:38:00, https://www.youtube.com/watch?v=aCND6VjXjAI.

14- "Negative Racial Stereotypes and Their Effect on Attitudes Toward African-Americans - Scholarly Essays - Jim Crow Museum." n.d. Jim Crow Museum of Racist Imagery. Accessed June 21, 2023. https://jimcrowmuseum.ferris.edu/links/essays/vcu.htm.

15- Stowe, Harriet Beecher. 2003. *Uncle Tom's Cabin*. New York. Harper & Row. Incorporated, reprinted 1965. Print. p 76-77.

16- Ibid. 165, 167

17- Clarissa, Aaron. "Uncle Tom's Failure." The Gilder Lehrman Institute. Web. Jan. 24, 2023.

18- Ibid. 17.

19- Ibid. 17.

# Chapter Nine

# What You Didn't Learn About Convict Leasing

1- Blackmon, Douglas A. 2009. *Slavery by Another Name*. Anchor. p. 18

2- "The Freedmen's Bureau | National Archives." 2016. National Archives. August 15, 2016. https://www.archives.gov/research/african-americans/freedmens-bureau.

3- "Assassination of Abraham Lincoln." n.d. Encyclopædia Britannica. Encyclopædia Britannica. Accessed June 21, 2023. https://www.britannica.com/event/assassination-of-Abraham-Lincoln.

4- "Why Land Redistribution to Former Slaves Unraveled After the Civil War | University of Virginia School of Law." 2019. University of Virginia School of Law. October 29, 2019. https://www.law.virginia.edu/news/201910/why-land-redistribution-former-slaves-unraveled-after-civil-war.

5- "Slave Codes - Encyclopedia of Arkansas." n.d. Encyclopedia of Arkansas. Accessed June 21, 2023. https://encyclopediaofarkansas.net/entries/slave-codes-5054/.

6- "13th Amendment to the U.S. Constitution: Abolition of Slavery (1865) | National Archives." 2021. National Archives. September 1, 2021. https://www.archives.gov/milestone-documents/13th-amendment.

7- "Digital History." n.d. UH - Digital History. Accessed June 21, 2023. https://www.digitalhistory.uh.edu/disp_textbook.cfm?psid=3179&smtid=2.

8- "Black Codes & Pig Laws | Themes | Slavery by Another Name | PBS." n.d. Slavery By Another Name. Accessed June 21, 2023. https://www.pbs.org/tpt/slavery-by-another-name/themes/black-codes-and-pig-laws/.

9- Convict Lease System: Alabama Statistics. n.d. UH - Digital History. Accessed June 21, 2023b. https://www.digitalhistory.uh.edu/disp_textbook.cfm?smtid=2&psid=3179.

10- Ibid., 9.

11- Terrell, Ellen. 2021. "The Convict Leasing System: Slavery in Its Worst Aspects." Library of Congress Blogs. Library of Congress. June 17, 2021. https://blogs.loc.gov/inside_adams/2021/06/convict-leasing-system/.

12- Flasco, Kathleen. n.d. "Attica Prison Uprising - Zinn Education Project." Zinn Education Project. https://www.facebook.com/ZinnEducationProject/. Accessed June 21, 2023. https://www.zinnedproject.org/materials/attica-prison-uprising/.

13- Ibid., 12.

14- Ibid., 12.

15- "Attica Prison Uprising - Zinn Education Project." n.d. Zinn Education Project. https://www.facebook.com/ZinnEducationProject/. Accessed June 21, 2023. https://www.zinnedproject.org/materials/attica-prison-uprising/.

16- Haas, Jeffrey. 2011. *The Assassination of Fred Hampton.* Chicago Review Press. p. 156-7.

17- Ibid., 16., p. 158

18- Ibid., 16., p. 158

# Chapter Ten

## What You Didn't Learn About Slave Patrols

1- Spitzer, Stephen, "The Rationalization of Crime Control in Capitalist Society," Contemporary Crises 3, no. 1 (1979).

2- ekuonline. 2013. "The History of Policing in the United States, Part 1 - EKU Online." EKU Online. https://www.facebook.com/EKUOnline. June 25, 2013. https://ekuonline.eku.edu/blog/police-studies/the-history-of-policing-in-the-united-states-part-1/.

3- Platt, Tony, "Crime and Punishment in the United States: Immediate and Long-Term Reforms from a Marxist Perspective, Crime and Social Justice 18 (1982).

4- Ibid., 3.

5- "Slavery, Institutional Racism, and the Development of State Surveillance as a Response to Resistance | Privacy SOS." 2014. Privacy SOS. July 29, 2014. https://privacysos.org/blog/slavery-institutional-racism-and-the-development-of-state-surveillance-as-a-response-to-resistance/.

6- Ibid., 5.

7- RUN NIGGER RUN, THE PATEROLLER CATCH YOU (RUN, NIGGER, RUN) sung by Joe Pat. Also found in Randolph, Vol. II, #264; Brown, Vol. III, #457.

8- Potter, Gary and Philip Jenkins, he City and the Syndicate: Organizing Crime in Philadelphia, Boston, Massachusetts, Ginn Press. 1985.

9- "Slavery, institutional racism, and the development of state surveillance as a response to resistance | Privacy SOS. 2014b. Privacy SOS. July 29, 2014. https://privacysos.org/blog/slavery-institutional-racism-and-the-development-of-state-surveillance-as-a-response-to-resistance/.

10- Ibid., 9.

11- Turner, K. B. , Giacopassi , D. , & Vandiver , M. (2006) . Ignoring the Past: Coverage of Slavery and Slave Patrols in Criminal Justice Texts. Journal of Criminal Justice Education, 17: (1), 181-195.

12- Ibid., 11.

13- "Office of Public Affairs |  Federal Jury Finds Three Men Guilty of Hate Crimes in Connection with the Pursuit and Killing of Ahmaud Arbery | United States Department of Justice." 2022. Department of Justice |  Homepage | United States Department of Justice. February 22, 2022. https://www.justice.gov/opa/pr/federal-jury-finds-three-men-guilty-hate-crimes-connection-pursuit-and-killing-ahmaud-arbery.

14- Ibid., 13.

15- Ibid., 13.

16- News. 2020. "Ahmaud Arbery: What You Need to Know about the Case - BBC News." BBC News. BBC News. May 11, 2020. https://www.bbc.com/news/world-us-canada-52623151.

17- Ibid., 16.

18- Service, Cnn Com Wire. 2020. "Derek Chauvin: What We Know about the Former Minneapolis Cop Charged in George Floyd's Death." The Mercury News. The Mercury News. June 1, 2020. http://www.mercurynews.com/2020/06/01/derek-chauvin-what-we-know-about-the-former-minneapolis-cop-charged-in-george-floyds-death/.

19- Birmingham, Alabama, erupted in chaos in 1963 when police aimed high-powered hoses and snarling dogs at Black men, women, and children protesters. Led by then-governor Eugene "Bull" Connor, the attacks lasted from May 2nd through May 10th and included police stepping on the neck of a Black woman, as Derek Chauvin would do to George Floyd some 57 years later.

20- "Office of Public Affairs | Former Minneapolis Police Officer Derek Chauvin Sentenced to More Than 20 Years in Prison for Depriving George Floyd and a Minor Victim of Their Constitutional Rights | United States Department of Justice." 2022. Department of Justice | Homepage | United States Department of Justice. July 7, 2022. http://www.justice.gov/opa/pr/former-minneapolis-police-officer-derek-chauvin-sentenced-more-20-years-prison-depriving.

21- "Desert Sun 28 December 1967 — California Digital Newspaper Collection." n.d. California Digital Newspaper Collection. Accessed June 23, 2023. https://cdnc.ucr.edu/cgi-bin/cdnc?a=d&d=DS19671228.2.19&e=------en--20--1--txt-txIN-------1.

## Chapter Eleven

## What You Didn't Learn About the State of Missouri v Celia

1- Colonial Virginia Laws on Slavery and Servitude (1639-1705) · SHEC: Resources for Teachers." n.d. · SHEC: Resources for Teachers. Accessed June 23, 2023. https://shec.ashp.cuny.edu/items/show/863.

2- "'Negro Womens Children to Serve According to the Condition of the Mother' (1662) - Encyclopedia Virginia." n.d. Encyclopedia Virginia. https://www.facebook.com/encyclopediava. Accessed June 23, 2023. https://encyclopediavirginia.org/entries/negro-womens-children-to-serve-according-to-the-condition-of-the-mother-1662/.

3- Wiltz, Allison. 2022. "The Scary Reason White People Keep Saying the Quiet Part Out Loud." Medium. June 27, 2022. https://readcultured.com/the-scary-reasonwhite-people-keep-saying-the-quiet-part-out-loud-c8827dac7181.

4- Hannah-Jones, Nikole and The New York Times Magazine. 2021. *The 1619 Project.* One World. Ibid., 4.p. 50.

5- Ibid., 4. p. 54.

6- User, Super. n.d. "Celia, A Slave, Trial (1855): Trial Testimony of Jefferson Jones." Famous Trials. Accessed June 23, 2023. https://famous-trials.com/celia/190-jonestranscript.

7- ———. n.d. "The Trial of Celia: A Chronology." Famous Trials. Accessed June 23, 2023b. https://famous-trials.com/celia/181-chronology.

8- Ibid., 7

9- "A Slave State of Missouri v. Celia: 1855 - Celia Speaks, The Trial Begins, On To The Missouri Supreme Court, Suggestions For Further Reading - JRank Articles." n.d. Wayback Machine. Accessed June 23, 2023. https://web.archive.org/web/20150715045955/http://law.jrank.org/pages/2539/State-Missouri-v-Celia-Slave-1855.html.

10- Ibid.

11- "Statement of Celia to Justice of the Peace June 25, 1855." Famous Trials. Accessed June 23, 2023b. https://famous-trials.com/celia/184-statement.

12- Ibid., 6.

13- King, Wilma. 2014. "'PREMATURELY KNOWING OF EVIL THINGS': THE SEXUAL ABUSE OF AFRICAN AMERICAN GIRLS AND YOUNG WOMEN IN SLAVERY AND FREEDOM." *The Journal of African American History*, no. 3 (July): 173–96. https://doi.org/10.5323/jafriamerhist.99.3.0173.

14- "Sexual Violence Targeting Black Women - Equal Justice Initiative Reports." n.d. Equal Justice Initiative Reports. Accessed June 23, 2023. https://eji.org/report/reconstruction-in-america/the-danger-of-freedom/sidebar/sexual-violence-targeting-black-women/.

15- Ibid., 13.

16- Wilson, Tony. 2021. "Malcolm X: 'The Most Disrespected Person in America, Is the Black Woman', Speech to Women - 1964 — Speakola." Speakola. Speakola. March 21, 2021. https://speakola.com/political/malcolm-x-speech-to-black-women-1962.

## Chapter Twelve

## What You Didn't Learn About Abraham Lincoln and Colonization

1- Abraham Lincoln." n.d. Encyclopedia Britannica. Encyclopedia Britannica. Accessed June 25, 2023. https://www.britannica.com/biography/Abraham-Lincoln.

2- "First Debate: Ottawa, Illinois - Lincoln Home National Historic Site (U.S. National Park Service)." n.d. NPS.Gov Homepage (U.S. National Park Service). Accessed June 25, 2023. https://www.nps.gov/liho/learn/historyculture/debate1.htm.

3- "Dred Scott v. Sandford (1857) | National Archives." 2021. National Archives. July 27, 2021. http://www.archives.gov/milestone-documents/dred-scott-v-sandford.

4- ———." 2021b. National Archives. July 27, 2021. http://www.archives.gov/milestone-documents/dred-scott-v-sandford.

5- Ibid., 1. "In this ruling, the U.S. Supreme Court stated that enslaved people were not citizens of the United States and, therefore, could not expect any protection from the federal government or the courts. The opinion also stated that Congress had no authority to ban slavery from a Federal territory."

6- Abraham Lincoln, "Address on Colonization to a Deputation of Negroes," Collected Works of Abraham Lincoln, vol. 5. University of Michigan Digital Library Production Services, 372-75, quod.lib.umich.edu/l/Lincoln/lincoln5/1:812?rgn=div1;view=fulltext.

7- Guyatt, Nicholas. 2016. "The American Colonization Society: 200 Years of the 'Colonizing Trick' | AAIHS." AAIHS. December 22,

2016. https://www.aaihs.org/the-american-colonization-society-200-years-of-the-colonizing-trick/.

8- Beard, Rick. 1345134654. "Lincoln's Panama Plan - The New York Times." Opinionator. 1345134654. https://archive.nytimes.com/opinionator.blogs.nytimes.com/2012/08/16/lincolns-panama-plan/.

9- "District of Columbia Emancipation Act 1862 | Constitution Center." n.d. National Constitution Center – Constitutioncenter.Org. Accessed June 26, 2023. https://constitutioncenter.org/the-constitution/historic-document-library/detail/district-of-columbia-emancipation-act-1862.

10- "Abraham Lincoln and the Politics of Black Colonization." n.d. U-M Library Digital Collections. Accessed June 26, 2023. https://quod.lib.umich.edu/j/jala/2629860.0014.204/--abraham-lincoln-and-the-politics-of-black-colonization?rgn=main;view=fulltext.

11- Ibid., 10.

12- Vorenberg, Michael. "Abraham Lincoln and the Politics of Black Colonization." *Journal of the Abraham Lincoln Association* 14, no. 2 (1993): 22-45. http://www.jstor.org/stable/20148897.

13- Hannah-Jones, Nikole and The New York Times Magazine. 2021. *The 1619 Project*. One World. p. 24.

14- Ibid., 8.

15- Ibid., 13.

16- "Emancipation Proclamation (1863) | National Archives." 2021. National Archives. August 16, 2021. https://www.archives.gov/milestone-documents/emancipation-proclamation.

17- Ibid., 16.

18- "Letter in Reply to Horace Greeley on Slavery and the Union—The Restoration of the Union the Paramount Object | The American Presidency Project." n.d. Welcome to The American Presidency Project | The American Presidency Project. Accessed June 26, 2023. https://www.presidency.ucsb.edu/node/342162.

19- Brown, DeNeen L. 2022. "Not All Enslaved Black People in Texas Were Freed on Juneteenth - The Washington Post." Washington Post. The Washington Post. June 19, 2022. https://www.washingtonpost.com/history/2022/06/19/juneteenth-texas-black-still-enslaved/.

20- bwbieltz. 2022. "Celebrating Juneteenth and What It Means | UNC-Chapel Hill." The University of North Carolina at Chapel Hill. https://www.facebook.com/uncchapelhill/. June 17, 2022. https://www.unc.edu/posts/2022/06/17/celebrating-juneteenth-and-what-it-means/.

21- McCullar, Emily. 2020. "How Leaders of the Texas Revolution Fought to Preserve Slavery – Texas Monthly." Texas Monthly. https://www.facebook.com/texas.monthly.magazine. October 29, 2020. https://www.texasmonthly.com/being-texan/how-leaders-texas-revolution-fought-preserve-slavery/.

22- "How the Black Codes Limited African American Progress After the Civil War | HISTORY." n.d. HISTORY. Accessed June 26, 2023. https://www.history.com/news/black-codes-reconstruction-slavery.

23- Blackmon, Douglas A. 2009. *Slavery by Another Name*. Anchor.

## Chapter Thirteen

## What You Didn't Learn About Black History Month

1- "Black History Month - African American Resource Center | CSUF." n.d. Achieve Greatness: California State University, Fullerton. Accessed June 26, 2023. http://www.fullerton.edu/aarc/historymonth/.

2- Racism, Encyclopedia of Race. n.d. "Association for the Study of Negro Life and History." Encyclopedia.Com | Free Online Encyclopedia. Encyclopedia.com. Accessed June 26, 2023. https://www.encyclopedia.com/social-sciences/encyclopedias-almanacs-transcripts-and-maps/association-study-negro-life-and-history.

3- "Kent State Community Reflects on How Black History Month Had an Impact on Their Lives | Kent State University." n.d. Kent Campus | Kent State University Kent State, One of Ohio's Leading Public Universities. Accessed June 26, 2023. https://www.kent.edu/today/news/kent-state-community-reflects-how-black-history-month-had-impact-their-lives.

4- "Willing to Sacrifice, Carter G. Woodson, the Father of Black History, and the Carter G. Woodson Home National Historic Site Historic Resource Study." *Woodson Home National Historic Site, Historic Resource Study*, vol. 1, April 2012, pp. iii-v.

5- Julius Rosenwald Fund (1917-1948): Amistad Research Center. *Julius Rosenwald Fund (1917-1948) | Amistad Research Center.* Retrieved on Jan. 20, 2023.

6- "The Man Who Built Sears & Roebuck : NPR." 2006. NPR. NPR. September 16, 2006. https://www.npr.org/2006/09/16/6085096/the-man-who-built-sears-roebuck.

7- "HEW News" Office of the Secretary, March 5, 1973; Memorandum "USPHS Study of Untreated Syphilis: the Tuskegee Study; Authority to Treat Participants Upon Termination of the Study," from Wilmot R Hastings to the secretary, March 5, 1973.

8- Minutes of the Julius Rosenwald Fund Executive Committee meeting, December 18, 1929, Records of the USPHS Venereal Disease Division, Record Group 90, National Archives, Washington National Record Center, Suitland, Maryland [hereafter NAWNRC].

9- Ibid., 8.

10- Vonderlehr, R.A., Clark, T., Wenger, O.C., Heller, J.R., Untreated Syphilis in the Male Negro, Journal of Venereal Disease Information. 17:260-265, (1936)

11- Jones, James H. 1993. *Bad Blood.* Simon and Schuster. p.71-73.

12- Miss Evers's character in Miss Evers Boys is loosely based on Nurse Eunice Rivers, a Black woman training at Tuskegee University. When the study began, she moved from John Andrew Hospital to work with Dr. Taliaferro Clark and Dr. Vonderlehr. Rivers gradually became the chief continuity person and was around for all forty years of the experiment. During the Great Depression, Blacks who could not afford healthcare joined Miss Rivers' Lodge, where they would get free physical exams at Tuskegee University, hot meals, and rides to and from the clinic.

13- Ibid., 11, Ch. 5, p. 73.

14- Charles Johnson Papers, Fisk University's interviews, numbered in sequence, for *Shadows of the Plantation* (Chicago, 1934). Interview #222, Box 556, CJP-FUA; Interview #231, Box 556, CJP-FUA

15- Jones, James H. 1993. *Bad Blood.* Simon and Schuster. p.64.

16- Ibid., 64.

17- Ibid., 70. Note: The problem of how to acquire these specially designed belts on a limited budget was solved by volunteer workers from the local chapter of the Red Cross who made them by the hundreds at a cost of only a few cents each.

18- Deuteronomy 28:32, "You will become an object of horror, ridicule, and mockery among all the nations to which YAH sends you."

19- "Apology For Study Done in Tuskegee." n.d. Welcome To The White House. Accessed June 26, 2023. https://clintonwhitehouse4.archives.gov/textonly/New/Remarks/Fri/19970516-898.html.

20- "A New African American Identity: The Harlem Renaissance | National Museum of African American History and Culture." n.d. National Museum of African American History and Culture. Accessed June 26, 2023. http://nmaahc.si.edu/explore/stories/new-african-american-identity-harlem-renaissance.

21- "We younger Negro artists who create now intend to express our individual, dark-skinned selves without fear or shame." Younge, Gary. 2002. "Renaissance Man of the South | Books | The Guardian." The Guardian. The Guardian. October 25, 2002. http://www.theguardian.com/books/2002/oct/26/featuresreviews.guardianreview36.

22- "THE HOPES AND TEARS OF 'HARLEM RENAISSANCE' - The Washington Post." 1989. Washington Post. The Washington Post. April 2, 1989. https://www.washingtonpost.com/archive/lifestyle/style/1989/04/02/the-hopes-and-tears-of-harlem-renaissance/266c9f16-2061-489a-997a-4d510521ff49/.

## Chapter Fourteen

## What You Didn't Learn About Lewis Howard Latimer

1- "Lewis Howard Latimer - Biography, Inventor, Draftsman." 2021. Biography. https://www.facebook.com/Biography. January 7, 2021. https://www.biography.com/inventors/lewis-howard-latimer.

2- Ibid., 1.

3- Ibid., 1.

4- Ibid., 1.

## Chapter Fifteen

## What You Didn't Learn about The Harriet Tubman (Mis)Quote

1- "Harriet Tubman - Harriet Tubman Byway." n.d. Harriet Tubman Byway. http://www.facebook.com/pages/Harriet-Tubman-Underground-Railroad-Byway/226184074095484. Accessed June 26, 2023. https://harriettubmanbyway.org/harriet-tubman/.

2- Ibid., 1.

3- "A Woman Called Moses (1978) - Turner Classic Movies." n.d. Watch Turner Classic Movies on TCM.Com. Turner Classic Movies. Accessed June 26, 2023. https://www.tcm.com/tcmdb/title/416023/a-woman-called-moses.

4- Imdb. Harriet (2019). https://www.imdb.com/title/tt4648786.

5- Ung, Jenny. 2018. "False Quote on Freed Slaves Wrongly Attributed to Harriet Tubman." AP News. October 4, 2018. https://apnews.com/article/archive-fact-checking-2312300417.

6- History, Captivating. 2021. *Underground Railroad.* Captivating History. p. 80.

7- Documenting the American South. Scenes in the Life of Harriet Tubman: Electronic Edition. Bradford, Sarah H. (Sarah Hopkins), b. 1818

8- Ibid., 7.

9- Ibid., 7.

10- Morgan, Robin. 2016. "Goodbye To All That #3 - Robin Morgan | Author, Activist, Feminist | NYC." Robin Morgan | Author, Activist, Feminist | NYC. https://www.facebook.com/TheRobinMorgan. November 28, 2016. https://www.robinmorgan.net/blog/goodbye-to-all-that-3/.

11- Ibid., 10.

12- "The Truths Behind the Myth of Harriet Tubman." n.d. Maxwell School. Accessed June 27, 2023. http://www.maxwell.syr.edu/news/article/the-truths-behind-the-myth-of-harriet-tubman.

13- Kate Clifford Larson, Bound for the Promised Land: Harriet Tubman: Portrait of an American Hero (New York: Ballantine Books, 2004), 275-276.

14- "6 Strategies Harriet Tubman and Others Used to Escape Along the Underground Railroad | HISTORY." n.d. HISTORY. Accessed June 27, 2023. http://www.history.com/news/underground-railroad-harriet-tubman-strategies.

15- "Harriet Tubman and the Underground Railroad (U.S. National Park Service)." n.d. NPS.Gov Homepage (U.S. National Park Service). Accessed June 27, 2023.

https://www.nps.gov/articles/harriet-tubman-and-the-underground-railroad.htm.

16- Brown, DeNeen L. 2021. "Harriet Tubman Was a Union Spy, Freeing Slaves during the Combahee River Raid in South Carolina - The Washington Post." Washington Post. The Washington Post. February 12, 2021.
https://www.washingtonpost.com/history/2021/02/08/harriet-tubman-spy-civil-war-union/.

17- History, Captivating. 2021. *Underground Railroad*. Captivating History.

18- "Harriet Tubman and the Underground Railroad - Bill of Rights Institute." n.d. Bill of Rights Institute. Accessed June 27, 2023. https://billofrightsinstitute.org/essays/harriet-tubman-and-the-underground-railroad

19- Harriet: The Moses of Her People. Text corrected and encoded by Natalia Smith First edition, 1995. Academic Affairs Library, UNC-CH. University of North Carolina at Chapel Hill, 1995.

20- ———. 2021b. "Harriet Tubman Was a Union Spy, Freeing Slaves during the Combahee River Raid in South Carolina - The Washington Post." Washington Post. The Washington Post. February 12, 2021.
https://www.washingtonpost.com/history/2021/02/08/harriet-tubman-spy-civil-war-union/.

21- "Facts : Harriet Tubman." n.d. Harriet Tubman. Accessed June 27, 2023. http://www.harriet-tubman.org/facts/.

## Chapter Sixteen

## What You Didn't Learn About Anna Murray Douglass

1- Fought, Leigh. 2018. "On the Life of Black Abolitionist Anna Murray Douglass | AAIHS." AAIHS. November 29, 2018. https://www.aaihs.org/on-the-life-of-black-abolitionist-anna-murray-douglass/.

2- "Frederick Douglass Papers: Family Papers, 1859-1903; Rosetta Douglass Sprague; 'Anna Murray Douglass, My Mother As I Recall Her,' 1900 | Library of Congress." n.d. The Library of Congress. Accessed June 27, 2023. https://www.loc.gov/item/mss1187900021/.

3- Ibid.

4- Boissoneault, Lorraine. 2018. "The Hidden History of Anna Murray Douglass | History| Smithsonian Magazine." Smithsonian Magazine. Smithsonian Magazine. March 5, 2018. https://www.smithsonianmag.com/history/hidden-history-anna-murray-douglass-180968324/.

5- Ibid., 2.

6- Fought, Leigh. 2018. "On the Life of Black Abolitionist Anna Murray Douglass | AAIHS." AAIHS. November 29, 2018. https://www.aaihs.org/on-the-life-of-black-abolitionist-anna-murray-douglass/.

7- Ibid.

8- Ibid., 2.

9- Douglass, Frederick, and Rosetta Douglass Sprague. *Frederick Douglass Papers: Family Papers, -1903; Rosetta Douglass Sprague; "Anna Murray Douglass, My Mother As I Recall Her," 1900*. 1900.

Manuscript/Mixed Material.
https://www.loc.gov/item/mss1187900021/.

10- Ibid., 6

11- Ibid., 6

## Chapter Seventeen

## What You Didn't Learn about These Unsung Women of The Harlem Renaissance

1- "Opportunity Magazine Is Published - African American Registry." n.d. African American Registry. https://www.facebook.com/africanamericanregistry/. Accessed June 27, 2023. https://aaregistry.org/story/opportunity-magazine-is-published/.

2- "Clarissa Scott Delany, Class of 1923 | Wellesley College." n.d. Wellesley College. Accessed June 27, 2023. https://www.wellesley.edu/davismuseum/whats-on/Virtual_platform/the-women-of-seed-to-harvest/node/180491.

3- "May Miller." n.d. Encyclopædia Britannica. Encyclopædia Britannica. Accessed June 27, 2023. https://www.britannica.com/biography/May-Miller.

4- "Marita Bonner | Villanova University." n.d. University | Villanova University. Accessed June 27, 2023. https://www1.villanova.edu/villanova/artsci/theatre/projects/aawp/bonner.html.

5- Atlas, Nava. 2018. "Dorothy West, Author of The Living Is Easy & The Wedding." Literary Ladies Guide. March 13, 2018. https://www.literaryladiesguide.com/author-biography/west-dorothy/.

## Chapter Eighteen

## What You Didn't Learn About the Chicago Black Renaissance

1- "The South Side - The Chicago Renaissance." n.d. Artsweb. Accessed June 27, 2023. https://artsweb.cal.bham.ac.uk/citysites/thesouthside/section04.htm.

2- "A Short Analysis of Gwendolyn Brooks's 'We Real Cool' – Interesting Literature." 2019. Interesting Literature. December 9, 2019. https://interestingliterature.com/2019/12/analysis-gwendolyn-brooks-we-real-cool/.

3- Ibid.

4- "Chicago Black Renaissance Movement." n.d. Accessed June 27, 2023. https://www.chicago.gov/content/dam/city/depts/zlup/Historic_Preservation/Publications/Chicago_Black_Renaissance_Literary_Movement_Report.pdf.

5- Ibid., 4.

## Chapter Nineteen

## What You Didn't Learn About Ida B. Wells-Barnett

1- "Ida B. Wells-Barnett | National Women's History Museum." n.d. National Women's History Museum. Accessed June 27, 2023. https://www.womenshistory.org/education-resources/biographies/ida-b-wells-barnett.

2- Ibid.

3- "Freedmen's Aid Society Records (Finding Aid) | Atlanta University Center." n.d. Atlanta University Center | Robert W.

Woodruff Library. Accessed June 27, 2023. http://radar.auctr.edu/islandora/object/auc.038%3A9999.

4- "Ida B. Wells: A Courageous Voice for Civil Rights - 2001-02." n.d. Home | Mississippi History Now. Accessed June 27, 2023. https://mshistorynow.mdah.ms.gov/issue/ida-b-wells-a-courageous-voice-for-civil-rights.

5- Ibid.

6- Ibid.

7- Ibid.

8- Ibid.

9- Ibid.

10- "The People's Grocery ... and Ida B. Wells." n.d. Historic Memphis in Vintage Photos. Accessed June 27, 2023. https://historic-memphis.com/biographies/peoples-grocery/peoples-grocery.html.

11- Ibid. 10.

12- "On May 27, 1892: White Mob Destroys Memphis Office of Ida B. Wells's Newspaper." n.d. | A History of Racial Injustice. Accessed June 27, 2023. https://calendar.eji.org/racial-injustice/may/27.

13- Ibid.

14- About - Ida B. Wells - LibGuides at The Westport Library." n.d. Home - LibGuides at The Westport Library. Accessed June 27, 2023. http://westportlibrary.libguides.com/IdaBWells.

15- "———." N.d. National Women's History Museum. Accessed June 27, 2023b. http://www.womenshistory.org/education-resources/biographies/ida-b-wells-barnett.

# Chapter Twenty

## What You Didn't Learn About Mary Beatrice Kenner

1- "Mary Beatrice Davidson Kenner | Lemelson." n.d. We Are Invention Education | Lemelson. Accessed June 28, 2023. https://lemelson.mit.edu/resources/mary-beatrice-davidson-kenner.

2- "Mary Beatrice Davidson Kenner – The Inclusive ScreenWriter." 2021. The Inclusive ScreenWriter. https://www.facebook.com/WordPresscom. May 11, 2021. https://theinclusivescreenwriter.com/mary-beatrice-davidson-kenner/.

3- Ibid., 1.

4- "The History of Menstrual Products – Aisle." n.d. Aisle. Accessed June 28, 2023. https://periodaisle.com/blogs/all/the-history-of-menstrual-products.

5- Bobier L. The Sexualization of Menstruation: On Rape, Tampons, and 'Prostitutes'. 2020 Jul 25. In: Bobel C, Winkler IT, Fahs B, et al., editors. The Palgrave Handbook of Critical Menstruation Studies [Internet]. Singapore: Palgrave Macmillan; 2020. Chapter 24. Available from: https://www.ncbi.nlm.nih.gov/books/NBK565624/ doi: 10.1007/978-981-15-0614-7_24

*Note:* *The first form of the maxi pad before Kenner's invention was invented by Johnson and Johnson in 1896. Sold as "Lister's Towels" or "Sanitary Napkins for Ladies," they didn't last long because tight advertising restrictions stopped the pads from being marketed. The product failed and was discontinued.*

# Chapter Twenty-One

## What You Didn't Learn about Phillip Downing

1- Kirby, Hilary. 2015. "The Life of a Song: 'I Heard It Through the Grapevine' | Financial Times." Financial Times. Financial Times. October 23, 2015. https://www.ft.com/content/9609a636-7743-11e5-933d-efcdc3c11c89.

2- Turner, Patricia Ann. 1993. *I Heard It Through the Grapevine*. University of California Press

3- Mahoney, Eleanor. 2017. "Philip B. Downing (1857-1934)." Black Past. October 31, 2017. https://www.blackpast.org/african-american-history/downing-philip-b-1857-1934/.

4- Walker, Ezekiel J. 2022. "Black Inventor Philip Downing Is the Reason for Mailboxes and Then Some." The Black Wall Street Times. https://www.facebook.com/TheBWSTimes. February 18, 2022. https://theblackwallsttimes.com/2022/02/18/black-inventor-philip-downing-is-the-reason-for-mailboxes-and-then-some/.

5- Ibid.

6- "Pioneers of Transportation - Metro Transit." n.d. Home - Metro Transit. Accessed June 28, 2023. https://www.metrotransit.org/pioneers-of-transportation.

7- Ibid., 4.

8- Ibid., 4.

# Chapter Twenty-Two

## What You Didn't Learn About the Brown Paper Bag Test

1- Nittle, Nadra Kareem. 2011. "The Roots of Colorism, or Skin Tone Discrimination." ThoughtCo. ThoughtCo. July 25, 2011. https://www.thoughtco.com/what-is-colorism-2834952.

2- Ibid.

3- Emenaha, Uchenna, and Nabeela Siddeeque. 2022. "Racial Passing – Showing Theory to Know Theory." Open Library Publishing Platform – Pressbooks for Ontario's Postsecondary Educators. Showing Theory Press. February 28, 2022. https://ecampusontario.pressbooks.pub/showingtheory/chapter/racial-passing/.

4- Ibid., 1.

5- "Jack and Jill: Elitist, Effective, Either, Neither, or Both? | New Pittsburgh Courier." 2019. New Pittsburgh Courier. January 29, 2019. https://newpittsburghcourier.com/2019/01/29/jack-and-jill-elitist-effective-either-neither-or-both/.

6- Ibid.

7- "National Survey of Black Americans, 1979-1980." n.d. Home Page. Inter-university Consortium for Political and Social Research [distributor]. Accessed June 28, 2023. https://doi.org/10.3886/ICPSR08512.v1.

8- Ibid.

9- Ibid.

10- Louis, Henry, and Cornel West. 1997. *The Future of the Race*. Vintage.

11- Staples, Brent. 1219437391. "As Racism Wanes, Colorism Persists - The New York Times." The New York Times Web Archive. 1219437391. https://archive.nytimes.com/theboard.blogs.nytimes.com/2008/08/22/as-racism-wanes-colorism-persists.

12- Wyatt, Heather Barbour. 2020. "The 'Brown Paper Bag Test' [Racial Bias] | Ongig Blog." Ongig Blog. Ongig. July 29, 2020. https://blog.ongig.com/diversity-and-inclusion/brown-paper-bag-test/.

13- Reddout, Jordan, Hickey, Gus, writers. Biermann, Todd, director. *Mixed-Ish*. Season #2, episode #1. "Sweet Child O' Mine." Jan. 26, 2021. Hulu.

14- *The Willie Lynch Letter*. 1999. p. 9. Frontline Distribution International.

15- Linné, Carl. 1964. *Carolus Linnaeus Systema Naturae, 1735*. Note: Racist whites classified humans in what is now known as race using Linnaean taxonomy, a system of scientific classification of plants and animals. Swedish naturalist Carolus Linnaeus created it with his 1735 publication of *Systemae Naturae*, a system of biological categories.

## Chapter Twenty-Three

## What You Didn't Learn About the Fultz Sisters

1- "Quadruplet Girls Born to N.C. Negro Couple," *Asheville Citizen-Times*, May 24, 1946.

2- Lorraine Ahearn, "Four Sisters, One Love," *News & Record* (Greensboro, NC), August 8, 2002, http://www.greensboro.com/four-sisters-one-love/article_cdccc43cbd23-5e85-931f-2ad69c4a1f40.html; and Jerry Bledsoe, *Bitter Blood* (New York, E. P. Dutton, 1988), 184–85.

3- Ibid.

4- Freeman, Andrea. 2019. *Skimmed*. Stanford University Press.

5- Raymond A. Bauer and Scott M. Cunningham, "The Negro Market," *Journal of Advertising Research* 10, no. 2 (April 1970): 9–11.

6- "PET Milk | Our History." n.d. PET Milk | Home. Accessed June 28, 2023. https://www.petmilk.com/history.

7- Ibid.

8- Lorraine Ahearn, "Four Sisters, One Love," *News & Record* (Greensboro, NC), August 8, 2002, http://www.greensboro.com/four-sisters-one-love/article_cdccc43c-bd23-5e85-931f-2ad69c4a1f40.html; and Jerry Bledsoe, *Bitter Blood* (New York, E. P. Dutton, 1988), 184–85.

9- Ibid.

10- Wood, Shelley. 2019. "The Dionne Quintuplets as a Cautionary Tale for Kidfluencers | Time." Time. Time. March 20, 2019. https://time.com/5555131/dionne-quintuplets-kidfluencers/.

11- Ibid., 8.

12- Ibid.

13- Tonya Mosley. *Here and Now.* How Black Women Were 'Skimmed' By Infant Formula Marketing. https://www.wbur.org/hereandnow/2019/12/16/skimmed-black-women-formula-marketing.

14- Kimberly Seals Allers, *The Big Letdown: How Medicine, Big Business, and Feminism Undermine Breastfeeding* (New York: St. Martin's Press, 2017), 14–16.

## Chapter Twenty-Four

## What You Didn't Learn About Rosa Parks Predecessors

1- "Rosa Parks: Bus Boycott, Civil Rights & Facts." n.d. HISTORY. Accessed June 28, 2023. https://www.history.com/topics/black-history/rosa-parks.

2- "The Rise and Fall of Jim Crow . Jim Crow Stories . The Scottsboro Case | PBS." n.d. THIRTEEN - New York Public Media. Accessed June 28, 2023. https://www.thirteen.org/wnet/jimcrow/stories_events_scotts.html.

3- Theoharis, Jeanne. 2021. *The Rebellious Life of Mrs. Rosa Parks (Adapted for Young People)*. Beacon Press.

4- Moon, Josh. "Bus Boycott took planning, smarts." Montgomery Advertiser. https://www.montgomeryadvertiser.com/story/news/local/blogs/moonblog/2015/11/29/bus-boycott-took-planning-smarts/76456904/.

5- "Social Welfare History Project  Jim Crow Laws and Racial Segregation." 2011. Social Welfare History Project. January 20, 2011. https://socialwelfare.library.vcu.edu/eras/civil-war-reconstruction/jim-crow-laws-andracial-segregation/.

6- Ibid.

7- "On Jul 16, 1944: Irene Morgan Arrested in Virginia For Refusing To Give Up Seat For White Passenger." n.d. | A History of Racial Injustice. Accessed June 28, 2023. https://calendar.eji.org/racial-injustice/jul/16.

8- "Congress of Racial Equality (CORE) | The Martin Luther King, Jr., Research and Education Institute." 2017. The Martin Luther King, Jr., Research and Education Institute. April 25, 2017. https://kinginstitute.stanford.edu/encyclopedia/congress-racial-equality-core.

9- "Transportation Inequity in the United States: A Historical Overview." n.d. American Bar Association. Accessed June 28, 2023. https://www.americanbar.org/groups/crsj/publications/human_rights_magazine_home/human_rights_vol34_2007/summer2007/hr_summer07_brenma/.

10- Katz, Brigit. 2021. "Civil Rights Pioneer Claudette Colvin Is Fighting to Clear Her Record | Smart News | Smithsonian Magazine." Smithsonian Magazine. Smithsonian Magazine. October 28, 2021. http://www.smithsonianmag.com/smart-news/claudette-colvin-who-was-arrested-for-refusing-to-give-up-her-bus-seat-in-1955-is-fighting-to-clear-her-record-180978959/.

11- Ibid.

12- Ibid.

13- Ibid.

14- Ibid.

15- "Browder, Aurelia S. - Civil Rights Digital Library." n.d. Civil Rights Digital Library. Accessed June 28, 2023. https://crdl.usg.edu/people/browder_aurelia_s.

# Chapter Twenty-Five

# What You Didn't Learn About Dr. Martin Luther King Jr.

1- Willie Christine (1927), Michael Jr. (1929), and Alfred Daniel (1930)

2- Martin Luther King, Jr. Research and Education Institute at Stanford https://kinginstitute.stanford.edu/

3- Nancy Clanton. Black History: Why Martin Luther King Jr.'s father changed their names. The Atlanta-Journal Constitution. Jan 13, 2023. https://www.ajc.com/lifestyles/why-martin-luther-king-father-changed-their-names/5ClNJ60MUtgsAZyCB4A4IN/

4- DeNeen L. Brown. "MLK's Name Change: How Martin Luther King Jr. was born Michael King Jr." The Washington Post. Jan 15, 2019. https://www.washingtonpost.com/history/2019/01/15/story-how-michael-king-jr-became-martin-luther-king-jr/

5- Mrs. King graduated from NEC in 1954 where she completed her degree in music education. An accomplished soprano, she received an Honorary Doctor of Music from NEC in 1971 and a Distinguished Alumni Award in 2004. In addition, she gave commencement speeches in 1971 and 2004 at the Conservatory. New England Conservatory: necmusic.edu/news/nec-unveils-bust-coretta-scott-king

6- Richard Wright. *12 Million Black Voices*. Basic Books; Reprint edition (December 16, 2002) Original Publishing: 1941. p. 104-111.

7- Richard Rothstein. *The Color of Law: A Forgotten History of How Our Government Segregated America*. Liveright Publishing Corporation. A Division of W.W. Norton & Company. New York. 2017.

8- Ibid., 7.

9- Ibid., 7.

10- MLK Quote. Martin Luther King Jr.'s 1966 Chicago Campaign. https://www.chicagomag.com/Chicago-Magazine/August-2016/Martin-Luther-King-Chicago-Freedom-Movement/

11- Ibid., 10.

12- MLK Quote. King's Vision: The Poor People's Campaign of 1967-68. www.poorpeoplescampaign-va.org/index.php/take-action/item/2-dr-king-s-vision-the-poor-people-s-campaign-of-1967-68

13- Poor People's Campaign: It's Time to Resist and Rise Above. Radical Discipleship. Apr 16, 2018. https://radicaldiscipleship.net/2018/04/18/poor-peoples-campaign-its-time-to-resist-and-rise-above/.

14- Ibid., 12.

15- Ibid., 13.

16- Washington Poor People's Campaign. "King's Legacy: The Original PPC." Washingtonppc. https://www.washingtonppc.org/king-s-legacy-the-original-ppc.

17- Honey, Michael. "Remembering Echol Cole and Robert Walker." *The Stand.* 1 Feb. 2018. www.thestand.org/2018/02/remembering-echol-cole-and-robert-walker/

18- Lockhart, P.R. The Memphis sanitation workers strike and MLK's unfinished fight for economic justice. 4, April 2018. www.vox.com/identities/2018/2/12/17004552/mlk-memphis-sanitation-strike-poor-peoples-campaign

19- Rodney Reed. "Sigma Pi Phi Fraternity, The Boulé: A Brief Overview (1904- )." Oct 13, 2020. https://www.blackpast.org/african-american-history/sigma-pi-phi-fraternity-the-boule-a-brief-overview-1904/

20- Ibid., 19.

21- Bates, Grigsby, Karen. "Elite Fraternity Widens Agenda for Black Men : Organizations: At the prompting of a younger generation, the prosperous and prominent members of the once-secret Boule are focusing more on social activism." Los Angeles Times. July 7, 1990.

22- Oldenburg, Don. "Tippy-Top Secret." The Washington Post. 4, Apr, 2004. https://www.washingtonpost.com/archive/lifestyle/2004/04/04/tippy-top-secret/09d44db5-3de4-4960-8f64-0e1ef57d6c95/

23- Ibid., 21.

24- Bates, Grigsby, Karen. "Elite Fraternity Widens Agenda for Black Men : Organizations: At the prompting of a younger generation, the prosperous and prominent members of the once-secret Boule are focusing more on social activism." Los Angeles Times. July 7, 1990.

25- A Guide to the W.E.B. Dubois Collection, 1867-1963. Fisk University Archives. Uzoma O. Miller Archival Assistant by Allyse Zanders, May, 2008. https://www.fisk.edu/wp-content/uploads/2020/06/du-boiswilliamedwardburghardtcollection1832-1963.pdf

26- The Martin Luther King Jr. Research and Education Institute. Standford University. Vietnam War. https://kinginstitute.stanford.edu/encyclopedia/vietnam-war

27- Chicago Defender. Steve Cokely Archives. https://chicagodefender.com/tag/steve-cokely/

28- Grossman, Ron. "The tense months before Martin Luther King Jr.'s assassination." (Apr 1, 2018). *The Chicago Tribune.* https://www.chicagotribune.com/opinion/commentary/ct-perspec-flash-mlk-king-assassination-0401-20180327-story.html

29- Harry Belafonte - kinginstitute.stanford.edu/king-papers/documents/harry-belafonte-0

30- Ibid., 27

Presbyterian News Service. MLK Weekend: A Call to Action. 13 Jan 2017. https://pres-outlook.org/2017/01/mlk-weekend-call-action/

## Chapter Twenty-Six

## What You Didn't Learn About A.D. King

1- Berstein, Jonathan. "This 1969 Music Fest Has Been Called 'Black Woodstock.' Why Doesn't Anyone Remember?" *Rolling Stone.* 9 Aug. 2019. www.rollingstone.com/music/music-features/black-woodstock-harlem-cultural-festival-history-859626/

2- The Martin Luther King, Jr. Research and Education Institute. King, Alfred Daniel Williams. https://kinginstitute.stanford.edu/encyclopedia/king-alfred-daniel-williams

3- Ibid., 2.

4- Ibid., 2.

5- Ibid., 2.

6- Ibid., 2.

7- Suggs, Ernie. "Younger brother gets lost in the shadow of Martin Luther King." The Seattle World. 20, Jan. 2014. www.seattletimes.com/nation-world/younger-brother-gets-lost-in-the-shadow-of-martin-luther-king/

8- Ibid., 7.

9- Notable Kentucky African Americans Database. "King, Alfred Daniel Williams." https://nkaa.uky.edu/nkaa/items/show/21.

10- Ibid., 1.

11- Ibid., 1.

12- Ibid., 7.

13- Ibid. 7.

## Chapter Twenty-Seven

## What You Didn't Learn about Robert Taylor

1- Grossman, James R. *Land of Hope: Chicago, Black Southerners, and the Great Migration.* 1989. Lemann, Nicholas. *The Promised Land: The Great Black Migration and How It Changed America.* 1991.

2- Ibid., 1.

3- Ibid., 1.

4- Welsh, H. N. "Racially Restrictive Covenants in the United States: A Call to Action." deepblue.lib.umich.edu/bitstream/handle/2027.42/143831/A_12%20Racially%20Restrictive%20Covenants%20in%20the%20US.pdf

5- Ibid., 4.

6- Housing and Race in Chicago. Chicago Public Library. https://www.chipublib.org/housing/

7- Mick Dumke, ProPublica, Haru Coryne, ProPublica, and Mariam Elba, ProPublica. "What's Gone Wrong At Chicago's Last Black-Owned Bank?" Block Club Chicago. 21 Dec., 2021. blockclubchicago.org/2021/12/21/whats-gone-wrong-at-chicagos-last-black-owned-bank

8- Modica, Aaron. "Robert Rochon Taylor (1899-1957)". *Black Past*. Dec. 9, 2009. https://www.blackpast.org/african-american-history/taylor-robert-rochon-1899-1957/

9- Ibid., 7.

10- Ibid., 7.

11- Weiss, Ellen (2011). *Robert R. Taylor and Tuskegee: An African American Architect Designs for Booker T. Washington*. Montgomery: NewSouth Books. pp. 137-138. ISBN 978-1-58838-248-1.

12- Lemann. N. "Four Generations in the Projects." New York Times Magazine. 13, Jan. 1991. https://www.nytimes.com/1991/01/13/magazine/four-generations-in-the-projects.html

13- Ibid., 8.

14- Kowski, A. "Home Histories: Robert Taylor Homes." 3, Feb. 2015 https://southsideweekly.com/home-histories-robert-taylor-homes/

15- Ibid., 14.

16- Ibid., 14.

17- Cherlise, R. "A look back at Chicago's Public Housing." *Chicago Reade.* 1 June, 2016. chicagoreader.com/blogs/a-look-back-at-chicagos-public-housing/

## Chapter Twenty-Eight

## What You Didn't Learn About The Black Panther Party for Self-Defense

1- **Red Summer of 1919:** "Racial tensions across the U.S. were exacerbated by the discharge of millions of military personnel back to their homes and domestic lives following the end of the war. Competition for opportunities in postwar America combined with a radically changed social landscape placed Whites and Blacks in conflict with one another, leading to tragic results. By the summer of 1919, approximately 500,000 African Americans had resettled in northern cities. In many cases, northern Whites—many of them newly arrived immigrants themselves—did not welcome Black newcomers. A four-day riot in Washington, D.C. began on July 19 when a rumor that Black men had assaulted a white woman incited mobs to attack local Black neighborhoods and assault random African American individuals on the streets. Off-duty sailors and recently discharged Army veterans led the mobs."
https://www.theworldwar.org/learn/about-wwi/red-summer

2- **Slums:** Slums were found in every major urban region of the United States throughout most of the 20th century, long after the Great Depression. In the late nineteenth century, the size and number of poverty-stricken slums in American cities exploded at an alarming rate. These slums had grown out of the country's rapid transformation into an industrial power following the American Civil War, the massive wave of unskilled European immigrants, and the millions of Southern Blacks arriving in need of jobs. The conditions in which slum dwellers lived were crowded, unsanitary, dangerous, and often without access to basic amenities like electricity or clean water. Evidence of people living in this type of filth could be found in nearly every major city, yet it was almost never mentioned in the media. Most of these slums had been ignored by the cities and states which encompassed them.

3- Moynihan, Michael. "Whitewashing the Black Panthers." Daily Beast. 12, July 2017. https://www.thedailybeast.com/whitewashing-the-black-panthers

4- Marxist History: USA: Black Panther Party: Ten Point Program https://www.marxists.org/history/usa/workers/black-panthers/1966/10/15.htm

5- "We Want Freedom. We Want Power To Determine The Destiny Of Our Black Community. We believe that Black people will not be free until we are able to determine our destiny." Point One in The Ten Point Program. Ibid.,4

6- Milkman, Arielle. "The Radical Origins of Free Breakfast for Children." *Eater.* 16 Feb. 2016. https://www.eater.com/2016/2/16/11002842/free-breakfast-schools-black-panthers

7- Ibid., 6

8- Ibid., 6

9- Black Panther Party's Free Breakfast Program (1969-1980). Jul 23, 2020. https://www.blackpast.org/african-american-history/black-panther-partys-free-breakfast-program-1969-1980/

10- The Radical Origins of Free Breakfast for Children. Eater. Feb. 16, 2016. https://www.eater.com/2016/2/16/11002842/free-breakfast-schools-black-panthers.

11- Medicare and Medicaid Act (1965). National Archives. Milestone Documents. https://www.archives.gov/milestone-documents/medicare-and-medicaid-act

12- Medicare and Medicaid Act (1965). National Archives and Records Administration. https://www.archives.gov/milestone-documents/medicare-and-medicaid-act.

13- Stories and histories BLACK PANTHER PARTY'S FREE MEDICAL CLINICS 1969-1975. BLACK PANTHER PARTY'S FREE MEDICAL CLINICS 1969-1975 - We Africa Preview. https://wap.org.ng/read/black-panther-partys-free-medical-clinics-1969-1975/.

14- Black Panthers and the importance of public health advocacy. Adewole S. Adamson, MD, MPP. Aug. 14, 2019. https://adeadamson.com/blog/2016/12/4/c7m74yvyuezl9wm4ea8ahay7vei36r.

15- A Huey P. Newton Story - Actions – COINTELPRO. PBS. https://www.pbs.org/hueypnewton/actions/actions_cointelpro.html.

16- Desert Sun, Volume 42, Number 296, 16 July 1969. Desert Sun 16 July 1969 - California Digital Newspaper Collection. https://cdnc.ucr.edu/?a=d&d=DS19690716.2.89&e=-------en--20--1--txt-txIN--------1.

17- Haas, Jeffrey. *The Assassination of Fred Hampton: How the FBI and the Chicago Police Department Murdered a Black Panther.* Chicago Illinois: Lawrence Hill Books, 2010 (hardcover), 2011 (paperback).

# Chapter Twenty-Nine

## What You Didn't Learn About the Events of September 15, 1963

1- Birmingham in the 1950s and 60s was known as the most segregated city in the United States. Jim Crow laws separated black and white people in parks, pools and elevators, at drinking fountains and lunch counters. African Americans were barred from working at the same downtown businesses where many of them shopped.

2- Gray, J. "Bombingham: Racist Bombings Captured in Chilling Photos." *Alabama.com.* 19, Feb. 2020. www.al.com/news/erry-2018/07/f39190a3553390/bombingham.html

3- Elliot, D. "Remembering Birmingham's 'Dynamite Hill' Neighborhood." NPR.org. 6 July, 2013. www.npr.org/sections/codeswitch/2013/07/06/197342590/remembering-birminghams-dynamite-hill-neighborhood

4- Ibid., 3.

5- Copeland, L. "A Martyr Gains History's Embrace." USA Today. 3 May, 2004. usatoday30.usatoday.com/news/nation/2004-05-03-birmingham_x.htm

6- Ibid., 5.

7- Johnson, C. "Johnny's Death: The Untold Tragedy In Birmingham." NPR. 15, Sept. 2010. www.npr.org/2010/09/15/129856740/johnnys-death-the-untold-tragedy-in-birmingham

8- Ibid., 7.

9- Gordon, K. R. "FBI Opens 3 Civil Rights Cold Cases." *AL.com.* 24, Nov. 2009. ww.al.com/birmingham-news-stories/2009/11/fbi_opens_3_civil_rights_cold.html

## Chapter Thirty

## What You Didn't Learn about Louis Till

1- Emmett Till Memory Project. Argo Corn Products: How the Great Migration Shaped the Life of Emmett Till. https://tillapp.emmett-till.org/items/show/24

2- The Free Social Encyclopedia: https://alchetron.com/Louis-Till

3- NPR. "Emmett Till's Father Was Also Hanged: A New Book Tells His Story." Nov. 12, 2016. https://www.npr.org/2016/11/12/501622050/emmett-tills-father-was-also-hanged-a-new-book-tells-his-story

4- Ibid 3.

5- American Experience. "Mamie Till Mobley. https://www.pbs.org/wgbh/americanexperience/features/emmett-biography-mamie-till-mobley/

6- Ibid., 5.

7- John Edward Wilderman. "Emmett Till, His Father, and the Scars on America's Soul." *Esquire.* Oct 19, 2016. https://www.esquire.com/news-politics/a48989/black-and-white-case/

8- A History of Racial Injustice. https://calendar.eji.org/racial-injustice/aug/28.

9- Ibid., 8.

10- Jesi Taylor. "Emmett Till's Ring and the Personal Effects of Violence." https://jesitcruz.medium.com/emmett-tills-ring-and-the-personal-effects-of-violence-ce546b6e549c

11- Ruthie Mae Crawford testifies about Emmett: (2005). The Untold Story of Emmett Louis Till by Keith Beauchamp. [8:24-36] YouTube. https://youtu.be/4y1BAqOnhMM.

12- From the Jim Crow-era, "Reckless Eyeballing" was a law against Black men looking at white women. Black people, in general, were also not allowed to look white people directly in the eye.

13- Carolyn Bryant Trial Transcript, Sumner, Mississippi, Sept 19-23, 1955.
http://law2.umkc.edu/faculty/projects/ftrials/till/CarolynBryant.pdf

14- Alexis Hoag. African American Exclusion from Jury Service, Past and Present. Brooklyn Law School. 2020. https://brooklynworks.brooklaw.edu/cgi/viewcontent.cgi?article=2275&context=faculty See also. Jury-based Gender Exclusion. https://eji.org/report/race-and-the-jury/why-representative-juries-are-necessary/sidebar/gender-based-jury-exclusion/

15- Time. When One Mother Defied America: The Photo That Changed the Civil Rights Movement. Time Magazine. https://time.com/4399793/emmett-till-civil-rights-photography/

16- Ibid., 5.

17- Ibid., 5.

18- History.com Editors. "Emmett Till murderers Make Magazine Confession." 24, January 1956. www.history.com/this-day-in-history/emmett-till-murderers-make-magazine-confession

# Chapter Thirty-One

# What You Didn't Learn About Mostafa Hefny

1- Race and Ethnicity: The U.S. Census Bureau considers race and ethnicity to be two separate and distinct concepts. www.cosb.us/home/showpubliseddocument/5935/637356700118370000

2- Cultural Genocide: U.S. Government Forces Egyptian Nubians to be Classified as White and Not Black. Move on, Petition. sign.moveon.org/petitions/justice-for-an-indigenous

3- Ibid., 2.

4- Zafar, A. "Egyptian Immigrant Wants to be Reclassified as Black." Time. 7, Sept., 2012. https://newsfeed.time.com/2012/09/07/egyptian-immigrant-wants-to-be-reclassified-as-black/

5- US Department of Health and Human Services Office of Minority Health. "Explanation of Data Standards for Race, Ethnicity, Sex, Primary Language, and Disability." https://minorityhealth.hhs.gov/omh/browse.aspx?lvl=3&lvlid=54

6- Roberts, D. 1619 Project: A New Origin Story. New York. Penguin Random House. 2021. p. 47

7- Ibid., 4.

8- Nikole Hannah-Jones, Dorothy Roberts. *A New Origin Story: The 1619 Project*. Race. P.47

# Chapter Thirty-Two

## What You Didn't Learn About the Physical Appearance of the Ancient Israelites and Egyptians

1- Black Twitter roasts TODAY show for Queen Nefertiti reconstruction that looks like a white woman. thegrio.com/2018/02/06/nefertiti-today-show/

2- BEKERIE, AYELE. "Ethiopica: Some Historical Reflections on the Origin of the Word <italic>Ethiopia</Italic>." *International Journal of Ethiopian Studies* 1, no. 2 (2004): 110–21. http://www.jstor.org/stable/27828841.

3- Ancient Egypt: The Light of the World by Gerald Massey p. 251

4- Timothy Kendall. "Wonders of the African World." Black Kingdoms of the Nile. https://www.pbs.org/wonders/Episodes/Epi1/1_retel1.htm

5- Origin of the word Ethiopia. https://cs.mcgill.ca/~rwest/wikispeedia/wpcd/wp/e/Ethiopia.htm

6- Kemet. http://www.griffith.ox.ac.uk/gri/9kemet.html. Origin of the word Egypt. http://www.touregypt.net/featurestories/kmt.htm

7- Bible Tools. Greek/Hebrew Definitions. https://www.bibletools.org/index.cfm/fuseaction/Lexicon.show/ID/H2526/Cham.htm

8- Gerald Massey, *Egypt the Light of the World.* p. 256. 1881/04/07. Richard Burton to Gerald Massey.[66] Letters & Memoirs of Sir Richard Francis Burton. Volume 3: 1880 to 1924. Edited by Gavan Tredoux.

9- Sir Richard Francis Burton, a 19th-century English explorer, writer, and linguist in 1883, wrote to Massey, "You are quite right about the

'AFRICAN' origin of the Egyptians. I have 100 human skulls to prove it."

10- *The Natural History of Man:* "In their complex and many of the complexions and in physical peculiarities, the Egyptians were an 'AFRICAN' race" (p. 124-125).

11- The Black Roots of Egypt's Glory. https://www.washingtonpost.com/archive/opinions/1987/10/11/the-black-roots-of-egypts-glory/1c3faf74-331c-4cc1-a6a0-3535fa3e098a/

12- Oxford Encyclopedia of the Archaeology of Ancient Egypt. https://www.twcenter.net/forums/showthread.php?302894-The-African-Origin-of-Ancient-Egyptian-Civilization/page5

13- Ibid., 12.

14- Source Here

15- Exodus 1:15-22

16- Exodus 2:1-3

17- Acts 7:22-23, 30

18- Genesis 17:2-7

19- Rudolph R. Windsor. From Babylon to Timbuktu: A History of the Ancient Black Races Including the Black Hebrews. Lushena Books. 1969. P.

20- Genesis 14:13

21- Genesis 25:29-34

22- Genesis 32:28

23- The Wives of Jacob: Rachel, Leahe, Bilhah, Zilpha, Genesis Chapters 29-20

24- Genesis Chapter 16

25- Ishmael marries Egyptian woman: Genesis Chapter 21

26- Joseph interprets Pharaoh's dream. Genesis Chapter 41.

27- Joseph excuses himself from brothers. Genesis Chapter 43:42

28- Yah calls Egypt his son, Hos 11:1

29- 21: Matthew Chapter 2. Focus verses: 13-16

30- Matt. 2:12-15

# Afterword

1- National Novel Writing Month website https://nanowrimo.org/
2- This quote is attributed to many people, including Socrates who is credited with saying: "I am the wisest man alive, for I know one thing, and that is that I know nothing." https://grammarhow.com/a-wise-man-knows-that-he-knows-nothing/

Enjoyed this book?

Please add a short review on your platform of choice and let me know what you thought!

www.yecheilyahysrayl.com
@yecheilyah

www.ingramcontent.com/pod-product-compliance
Lightning Source LLC
Chambersburg PA
CBHW012034200426
43209CB00055B/1560